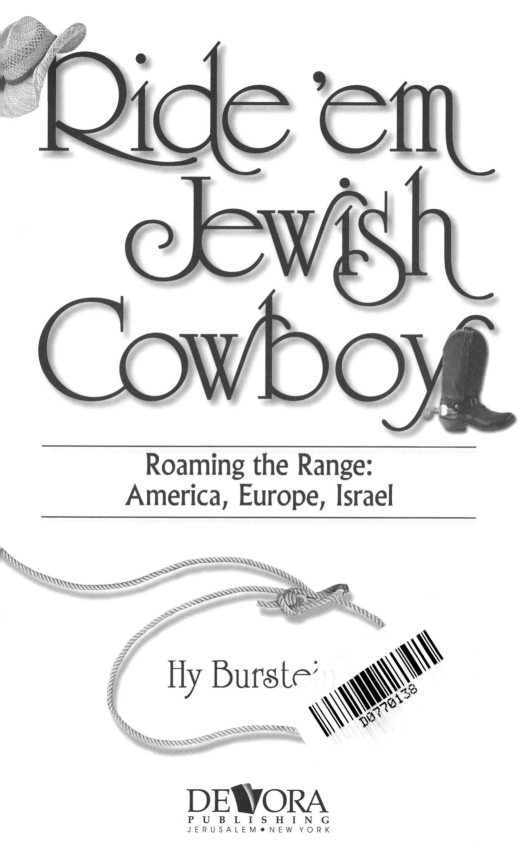

# Ride 'em Jewish Cowboy

Roaming the Range:
America, Europe, Israel

Hy Burstein

DEVORA
PUBLISHING
JERUSALEM ◆ NEW YORK

# Ride 'em Jewish Cowboy

Published by DEVORA PUBLISHING COMPANY

Text Copyright © 2004 Hy Burstein
Cover and Book Design: *Shlomo Benzaquen*
Editor: *Allison Schiller*

ISBN: 1-930143-95-8 (Hardcover)
ISBN: 1-932687-14-9 (Softcover)

E-mail: *sales@devorapublishing.com*
Web Site: *www.devorapublishing.com*

Printed in Israel

# Dedication

To my wonderful wife ZUZIK who has been my companion and inspiration at home and on the range.

# Table of Contents

The author as "Hy Jack", professional boxer, c. 1947

# Preface

While traveling for business by train to Louisville, Kentucky in 1952, I saw firsthand the racist policies against the blacks in America. It was also the first time I had seen *whites only* signs over public water fountains, toilets, doors or in the train station. On the trains themselves there were separate cars for whites and blacks. Toronto wasn't too far behind in name-calling: niggers, dagos, heebs and kikes.

In 1956, the large manufacturers of soft drinks, chocolates and ice cream purchased their sugar requirements in hundred pound cotton bags. Companies such as Coca-Cola, Neilson and Wrigley's used tens of thousands of sugar bags each week in the production of their food and beverage products. The demand for empty cotton sugar bags was high because often after the bags were used, they were washed, the print was removed, and they were sold in supermarkets as dish towels and wiping cloths. When they were sewn together, they made excellent inexpensive bed sheets

I recall sending my brother-in-law to a Wrigley's factory located on Carlaw Avenue in lower east Toronto where he would try to purchase empty cotton sugar sacks. After returning to the office he reported that a Mr. Clark asked him if was Jewish. My brother-in-law told him that he was. Mr. Clark replied that he didn't do business with Jews. When I heard all of this, my immediate thought was revenge. I called Mr. Clark, who I learned was the purchasing manager, and told him I was a farmer from Midhurst, Ontario and that I required cotton sacks to hold potatoes.

"Are you Jewish?" he exclaimed. He then carried on by asking what my name was.

"My name is Harry Kostin, and no, I am not Jewish," I replied. Mr. Clark then requested that I see him in his office as soon as possible. I didn't waste any time. I hurried out to east Toronto to Wrigley's executive offices. At the information desk I was told that Mr. Clark would see me. I was shown to his large private office. His appearance reminded me of a school teacher or possibly a bank manager.

He started the conversation, "So you're a farmer from Midhurst?"

Yes, Mr. Clark," I replied. "I farm 150 acres of potatoes, and I require bags to hold them."

"So why don't you purchase them from bag dealers?" he asked. "

I tried," I said, "but they want an arm and a leg and I can't afford the prices they are asking." We agreed on a price and Mr. Clark then set down the rules for purchasing the bags.

- Pickups were to be made each month.
- Terms of payment were C.O.D. to him in person.
- A receipt was to be mailed to my address in Midhurst.

After shaking hands on the deal, he asked again if I was Jewish. "Well, Mr. Clark, with a name like Kostin, what do you think?" I replied. After leaving his office I realized I had a problem. The payment receipt was to be mailed to an address that didn't exist.

Each month the routine for each pickup was the same. I would cover the name "Burstein Bags" on both doors of the truck. I would make my pickup of five to ten thousand sacks, and then I would go to the executive offices to see Mr. Clark. After taking the money he would begin inquiring about my past, present and future. He would also inquire about my marital status, my family life, the potato crops and the potato markets, etc... I am sure he wondered why all the mail containing my purchase receipts was being returned to him stamped "wrong address." On each of my visits I had to give him reasons why his mail wasn't getting through. One reason was possibly mistaken rural route numbers, I suggested. Finally Mr. Clark personally took a drive to Midhurst, and, of course, no one there had heard of Harry Kostin. Eventually he confronted me. I had to think fast, so I said "Mr. Clark, didn't I mention to you that I moved to Barrie, Ontario?" These storied excuses would be used again and again until a Barrie potato farmer by the name of Clarence Cumming, a long-time friend and customer of ours, suggested that I use his address. After two years of this cat-and-mouse game, I finally rented a forty-acre farm in Rexdale, Ontario and used it as my address. This location was not too far from the present Woodbine Racetrack and my legitimate address.

It wasn't long until Mr. Clark did some detective work, tracked me down and paid an unexpected visit to the farm. The day he chose to visit, my large truck was parked out front with the name "Burstein Bags" on both doors. Inside the farmhouse were my friend Ray Morphet and my girlfriend Frances Sherriff. As I saw him leaving his car, I told Frances quickly that she was now Mrs. Kostin, and that I'm a potato farmer. Mr. Clark stormed up the stairs of the porch, and before he could start knocking, I had the door open.

"What's that Jew truck Burstein Bag doing here? Is that your truck, Harry?" he exploded.

"Of course not, Mr. Clark," I coolly answered. "I purchase bags from that company, and they delivered them here, and their damn truck broke down." I then changed the subject by saying, "I want you to meet my wife, Frances." Satisfied with my explanation, he left shaking his head.

My next and last encounter with Mr. Clark was, of all places, at a hockey game at the Maple Leaf Gardens. He was with his wife, and I was with Frances. Sure enough, he spotted me out of 15,000 people and immediately insisted that I follow him to his home for tea. Since he would not take no for an answer, I accepted his invitation. On the way to his home, I briefed Frances on my predicament. Once again she was my wife, we had three children, and I was a potato farmer. Frances was born in the United Kingdom and still had a British accent, so she was quite convincing. Since Mr. Clark was from London, they hit it off, and by the time we left his home, he would have bet a million to one that I was a Christian potato farmer, married with children.

In October 1959, soon after I married Sara Elymor, Miss Israel, I returned to Toronto. Newspapers printed the photos of my wife and me in an article describing the wedding. "From Army to Honeymoon" read the headlines. The stories mentioned a Canadian from Toronto, a Mr. Harry Burstein, manager of his father's cotton bag business known as Burstein Bag Company. Can you imagine the shock Mr. Clark received when he saw my photo and the description of my business in the papers? Actually we continued to do business, but I sent my driver to make the pickups. This lasted a short time because Wrigley's moved their operations to a new, larger plant and installed huge silos to hold sugar in bulk, and they no longer needed to purchase their sugar in cotton sacks. Mr. Clark suffered a heart attack and retired not long after, in 1960.

# Introduction

Here is a story of a man with a passion. A passion for horses. His story traces a life of travelling around the world as a cowboy, a Jewish cowboy.

As we follow Hy Burstein through his adventures, we learn about his other passion, a greater passion. Hy Burstein also has a passion for being Jewish. As we learn about his life, we can see how he stood up against clashes of culture and direct anti-Semitism. We can see how the strength of horsemanship and the mettle of a cowboy helped this Jewish Cowboy face difficulties with a smile.

Hy Burstein was born in Toronto in 1928, the son of Russian immigrants, and has lived there all his life. His life story is one of adventure, adversity, love, success, triumpth and failure. Hy's early life tells of growing up and working in Toronto where anti-Semitism was encountered on an almost daily basis. Hy's story is a story of overcoming the stigma of being Jewish by thrusting himself into a world that was both alien and fascinating.

As a teenager, Hy trained as a boxer and began his career with a win over middleweight boxer, Harry Ramies. After five professional fights, his boxing career ended when Gord Wallace pummelled him in a fight that saw his eyebrows cut.

Hy followed his boxing career with a move into the saddle of a truck, another high-risk pusuit. He treated truck driving as a profession, and in 1954 won the Ontario Top Truck Driver Award in the eighth Canadian National Truck Rodeo held in Toronto. Hy had begun driving a truck while working for his father's burlap bag business. In 1968, Hy left the world of trucks to venture into business for himself, and became a successful businessman, building and expanding a plastics manufacturing business that is still in existence.

In 1959, after a whirlwind romance, he married Sara Elymor, Miss Israel of 1957, to whom he is still married. Soon after Sara's arrival in Canada, the couple moved to a one-hundred-acre farm outside Toronto city limits. We hear stories of their five sons who join him in his love of horses, and who continue to work with him in the family business. We also learn about Hy's daughter, who travels with him on horseback through Spain and Ireland.

But mostly we hear about horses. Ride 'em Jewish Cowboy is a story of a love of riding so profound that it carries this cowboy on adventures all over the world. The theme of challenging and succeeding in an alien world dominates Hy Burstein's life, and this is no more evident than in his riding adventures.

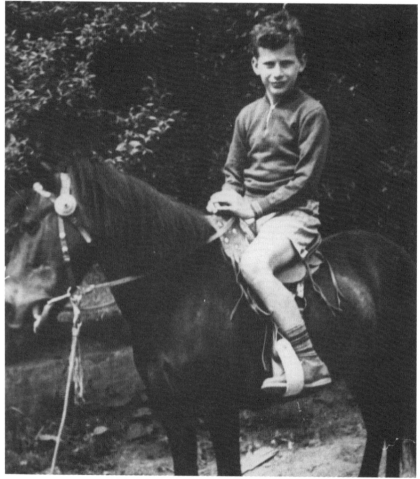

The author's first pony ride at age 7 – 1935

## Chapter 1

# Riding Hy

**M**y name is Hy Burstein, and some folks have called me Riding Hy. It's interesting to note that before becoming a traveling horseman, I first sat on a pony at the age of seven, probably costing my dad fifty cents for a photo back in 1935, deep in the Depression years. The next time I got on a horse was in 1942, when my older sister wanted me to join her and a few friends at the High Park Riding Academy located in Toronto across from Lake Ontario, near the present intersection of Parkside and Lakeshore Boulevards. I remember being quite frightened when the horse put his head down to eat some grass and there was no way I could pull his head back up. At fourteen years of age, with no riding experience or training, I admit, I wanted to jump off.

Four years later, in 1946, with World War II over, at the age of eighteen with a drivers license in hand, I convinced my dad to loan me his 1938 Model Ford, and I managed to get to the Circle M Ranch in outlying Kleinberg, fifteen miles northwest of Toronto, where you could rent horses by the hour or house your own horse and pay boarding fees. This was the first time I had ever seen privately owned horses, and I was amazed that people could actually afford to buy and ride their own horses. The Circle M Ranch stable was run by Al Greco, later known as the Colonel. The Circle M Ranch was a great place to ride and was also used as a movie studio for Western-style movies. The man who owned it was Charles Mavety, quite a wealthy businessman, the sole distributor of Hollywood films to all the movie houses in

Ontario. It was here that I vowed that one day I would purchase my own horse, which I would saddle and ride to my heart's content. Al Greco, who had worked for many years at the ranch, eventually opened his own ranch on a much smaller scale. He offered rides to the general public and eventually settled down on his ten-acre spread, where he opened a supply store that sold saddles and all sorts of tack and where he eventually bought and sold all types of saddle horses. In fact, I happened to purchase a few trailers and at least eight horses from the Colonel in the nineteen eighties and nineties for myself and for my children's use. In 1946 Circle M Ranch was the only decent place to rent a horse to ride. The countryside had space, hills, bush and a good choice of riding horse. Yes, it was far. The only way to get there was by car, and to drive in 1946 was something to be proud of, especially right after World War II.

Al passed away in 2000, and I miss him. He was a character, and it was an experience to deal with him. No matter how much we argued, we always came to terms. At the time, I rented from a close friend Riding Hy Ranch, a forty-acre farm, which had a small barn and brick home and was located two miles from Toronto. It was a place that as a single man of twenty-eight I enjoyed the freedom with friends for two years, riding horses, parties and living it up with my beautiful girlfriend, Frances.

In 1956, while driving along the newly opened 401 east/west highway, which at that time was the northern boundary of Toronto, in the area of Kipling and Martingrove, I noticed a large barn with a sign reading "Kingsview Farms."

The many times I drove by; I witnessed horses being ridden in the barnyard and a few horses being schooled in a large outdoor ring. After breaking up with my girlfriend Frances, I did what every red-blooded Canadian would do: I bought a dog and horse to help me through the lonely days and nights. It was at Kingsview Farms that my horse career started.

The owner of Kingsview Farms was an elderly gentleman by the name of Mr. John Menary, who made his millions in the Depression years by purchasing real estate when everyone was

1945

selling out. Mr. Menary had one son and a grandson, whose name was Ray Morphet.

I remember back in 1956, parking on the shoulder parallel to the barn and climbing the wooden rail fence. At that time Highway 401 was only four lanes wide. Upon entering the huge barn, I found two sections, one set up for cattle, but empty and

16

the other half, large box stables and standing stalls. All of the stalls were filled with horses, and an old timer with a broom in hand was sweeping the floor. He was Archie, a grumpy old man with a brush mustache and a once-in-a-lifetime character, who had his own sleeping quarters on the premises. Beside the barn and driving shed was a lovely country home where John Menary's grandson Ray lived with his wife, Audrey, and their three children. Ray was the manager of Kingsview Farms.

Old Man Menary was considered a tightwad and told me that he judged people by the cars they drove. The better, or more expensive the car, the higher the price he would charge for his horses.

I was relieved to hear that Kingsview Farms was open to the public and that you could board your horse there, but that it allowed no rentals. From the corner of my eye, I spotted an elderly gentleman, well dressed in a suit and tie, picking up some old cartons from the floor. I introduced myself after Archie told me that he was the owner. I mentioned that I was interested in purchasing a horse, and he asked me which style I rode, English or Western. Since up to now I was riding at the Circle M only in Western saddle, I replied Western.

"Do you prefer a Gelding stallion or a mare?" he inquired. "I've got a great Palomino mare you can buy for three hundred dollars, and you can board her and ride here and pay twenty five dollars monthly for a standing stall or thirty five dollars for a box stall ten feet by twelve feet. Its your choice," he said.

He then introduced me to his grandson Ray Morphet who would teach me the rules of the barn and assist me in acquiring a saddle, bridle and all the necessary supplies required in owning a horse.

Ray Morphet became very important in my life at this time. He taught me riding skills, jumping skills, handling, and overall care for horses. He was a top rider himself and very skilled at jumping and had won many ribbons and trophies throughout the horseshow circuit. Ray was a great guy who I admired. Both of us took a liking to each other and became close friends. Ray had

1947 – At the Ⓜ Ranch

one serious problem: he was an alcoholic. He drank heavily from lunch right through to midnight.

Up to this time in my life, I hadn't thought about drinking, but Ray Morphet certainly changed that. I drank more beer in one month with Ray than I ever had in twenty-eight years. For the next three years, I had the time of my life. Ray would invite me regularly to the new home that his grandfather had purchased for him in the upper-class Kingsway area, where we would spend hours drinking, joking and talking horse business. Eventually I noticed Ray not riding as often, turning his attention to consuming more alcoholic beverages other than beer like rye, scotch, gin and vodka. One evening at his home I said, "Ray, when will all this drinking end?" To which he replied sarcastically, "When I run out of money and friends."

"But Ray," I said, "that could happen sooner than you think."

Then with a bit of anger in his voice, he replied, "Let me worry about it. Let's drop the subject now!"

Through Ray I learned about loading and unloading horses and traveled to many horse shows, which I entered. Ray convinced me to trade in the Palomino mare (Golden Girl) and obtain instead a beautiful chestnut three-year-old gelding with four white stockings and a stripe down his nose.

I named him *Iron Lad,* and that started my jumping career, which was highlighted at the 1957 Royal Winter Fair. Over the next two years I eventually returned to my girlfriend Frances, whom I dated until I married my present wife in 1959. Ray and I broke up our friendship in 1961 after a disastrous business partnership in which the alcohol finally took over his life and left him in ruins. Ray lost his beautiful home that he moved into after his grandfather sold the hundred-acre Kingsview Farms. The last time I ever saw Ray was in my office in 1968. He gave me his cigarette lighter to hold as collateral for a $10 loan. I never saw him again. I know he died of liver disease before he reached his fifty-seventh birthday.

In 1958 John Menary sold a large portion of Kingsview Farms,

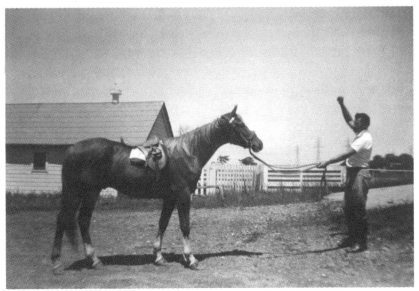

My first saddle horse, "Iron Clad" – 1956

19

Author on the right, Ray Mophet and Ran center, John McCrae left

including the barn, horses and all the farm sheds and buildings. He immediately purchased a hundred-acre farm approximately fifteen miles northwest of Toronto and just south of a village called Bolton. It had a large, clean barn that could hold up to fifteen horses. I moved my own horse there, and by then old Archie had died. Menary hired a fellow by the name of Al Peters, a good-natured guy with empty pockets but a big heart.

While riding near the stable I spotted a "For Sale" sign about a thousand feet south and across the dirt road. I noticed a good-sized creek running through the property, plus, the property was not flat, but hilly with many trees and quite attractive - a place I had always dreamed of owning.

I want to go back to 1959, when I was single and thirty-one years of age. I was self-employed, earning a good wage, drove a green convertible Cadillac and was totally fed up with my girlfriend of six years. My stepmother convinced me to visit Israel, and I did. At that time Israel had only been a state for eleven years, and Tel Aviv, where I spent most of my time, had but one major hotel, which was called the Dan, located on the Mediterranean. My reservation was for two weeks, and little did I realize that I would spend five weeks in Israel and return to Toronto a married man.

It was at the Dan Hotel that I was introduced to Ruth, an eighteen-year-old soldier in the Israeli army. She was quite attractive, and after a week of dating, I proposed marriage, and she accepted. I cabled my parents with the good news and, after meeting Ruth's parents, immediately made the wedding plans. In the following week, we double-dated with a friend of Ruth's and his date, Sara Elymor, also an eighteen year old and former Miss Israel beauty queen. She was enlisted in the navy and spoke little English. When I saw Sara, I knew immediately that I had made an error in my choice of Ruth, and as luck would have it, Ruth was called by her army unit to report to duty and had to leave Tel Aviv for at least one week.

One week was all I needed to convince Sara to marry me. That was the easy part. I still had to confront Ruth with the latest developments, and to do this, I rented a rowboat on the Yarkon

Author jumping

Hy Burstein's marriage to Sara Elymor (Miss Israel Beauty Queen) – Oct 13, 1959

River and broke the news to Ruth that I was not going to marry her. It was not an easy task.

The next obstacle to overcome was getting a marriage license. All marriages in Israel are controlled by the strict Orthodox rabbinate, which required me to prove that I was Jewish. That proof had to come from an Orthodox rabbi in Toronto, which required my father's assistance. Finally the wedding took place after asking Sara's father for her hand . No one from my family attended, and to be honest, I was nervous. After a three-day honeymoon in the beautiful Accadia Hotel in Herzliya on the Mediteranean, I returned to Toronto, and my bride followed three months later, after receiving her discharge from the navy.

She arrived in Canada on December 19 during a snowstorm, entering the bitter cold in Montreal. In 1960, I showed my wife the land that was for sale across from Menary, and I said I wanted to buy it and build our home there. Even though it was quite a lonely location, on a lightly traveled road in Albion Township and completely surrounded by farms in all directions, she said that if I wanted it, I should buy it. I did, and our new home was built and ready to move into by the latter part of 1961.

Our first-born, Sonny, made it the three of us. Oh, yes, and a German shepherd of six months that we called Wolf. In the summer of 1962, twin boys arrived as well as a five-year-old standard-bred Gelding I called Joe, who died at the ripe-old-age of thirty-six. That's right, he was one great horse who never let me down for thirty-one years. Actually Mr. Menary sold me Joe for three hundred dollars as he was preparing to ship him to the Toronto Police Mounted Division.

My favorite expression about Joe, who was boarded out at many stables during the sixties and seventies, in and around Toronto, was that if I had bought land wherever Joe dumped his manure, I might have landed up as one hell of a wealthy horseman.

My best horse ever "Old Joe" – Owned him over 30 years. Died of natural causes at 36

# Chapter 2

# The Horse, The Horse, The Horse

**How fortunate is the man who has a wife, a son and a horse.**

*– Arabian proverb*

There is a book that I read recently entitled *Wild About Horses*, written by Mr. Lawrence Scanlon, which I highly recommend horse lovers to read. In the book he explains how horses have, in one way or another entered into all of our lives. For example, watching or betting on standard and thoroughbred horse races, taking the family to see the rodeo where the bucking horse is king, and let us not forget the quarter-horse races or the performing horses at the circus where trained horses are put through their strides. Then there is the latest phenomenon, the medieval jousting live shows, where families can enjoy their dinners while watching the brave horsemen trying to knock each other off their steeds. Hundreds of movies have been made in Hollywood with thousands of performing horses carrying cowboys chasing Indians and vice-versa, soldiers fighting brave battles on horseback, whether General Custer at Little Big Horn in Montana or the Charge of the Light Brigade in 1854, during the Crimean War. Horses were used in battle in the American Civil War, the Boer War in South Africa and many others too numerous to mention, and they have worked their hearts out for the human race pulling logs from the forest or pulling wagons delivering bread, milk, ice and coal. Before the advent of the automobile, the Pony Express delivered the mail, and the stagecoach delivered passengers to their destinations. Horses were worked to death in coal mines, and during the Klondike Gold Rush in the far north, where more than three thousand pack horses died on the White Pass Trail from starvation, and many were badly loaded and died violently, losing their balance and plunging from the cliff's edge to the waters below. Many were just beaten to death by men trying vainly to urge them onward. Actually, the trail became known as the Dead Horse Trail. Horses also helped the farmers plow their fields and bring in their crops.

Though the horse is a powerful and brave animal, there are places and situations in which the horse cannot endure, and in a little-known piece of history, when the journalist Henry Stanley left Zanzibar for the east coast of Africa in his search for Dr. Livingston in 1871, two of his riding horses died after only three days on the African continent. Two famous Englishmen had something to say about the horse. A famous quote from Winston Churchill said, "No hour of life is lost that is spent in the saddle." The other from Lord Palmerston: "The best thing for the inside of a man is the outside of a horse." I believe in a horse-human bond. And after forty-six years of riding and caring for the horse, I can truly say the horse and I can communicate with each other.

I believe many improvements in horse training and breaking have occurred in the past decade. If you read Monty Roberts's, *The Man Who Listens to Horses*, you will understand how his method of breaking a horse can be attained in less than an hour in most cases, without cruelty, instead of three weeks of cruelty by his dad, Marvin Roberts. It's also a pleasure to watch the Royal Canadian Mounted Police perform their world famous Musical Ride, which I have witnessed many times.

However, I did not enjoy watching the Spanish and Mexican bull rings where horses are blindfolded and both sides of their bodies are covered with heavy, thick blankets to protect them from getting pierced by the sharp horns of the bull, who can actually lift the horses up and sometimes flip them right over on their sides. If the horse wasn't blindfolded, you can imagine the fear that would overtake the poor animal when the bull is provoked in various ways and eventually may charge the horse. I feel the main provocation comes when the picadors ride the blindfolded horses and start using their long spears to stab the bull's hump, causing the blood to gush out and at the same time weakening the animal and causing his head to drop. To make certain he gets a deep wound, the picador will stand up in his stirrups. This is the reason the horse is in constant danger from a most enraged bull.

There is a soft-cover book that was printed in 1996 by Mr. Arthur Sacks called *Worldwide Riding Vacations*. Following are a few excerpts from this interesting book dedicated to horse vacations:

> "The horses you find at equestrian vacation destinations are, for the most part, very well trained for their jobs. At a minimum, this means that the horses must be able to adjust to a variety of riders and their potentially inaccurate or confusing demands, created by poor balance, fear or inexperience. For those of you who wish or need to ride at a leisurely pace, you will find the horse well suited for the task. Their training and experience will help to guide you.

> "For those of you who like more excitement in your ride, finding the ideal horse becomes more difficult. The problems are two-fold, one relating to the quality of the horse and the other to the quality of the rider. A horse that is better suited for a more advanced pace is likely to be younger and more spirited and, because he is using his athleticism to a greater degree, much more prone to injury. This makes it difficult for the supplier to always have the ideal horse ready. An older trail horse, if frightened, is likely to take a half step and shift weight slightly, hardly the stuff to knock even an inexperienced rider to the ground. A more athletic horse, when frightened, may make a five step move, dip more radically, crow hop or rear – you may get dumped.

> "An experienced rider may want more from a horse than he or she may be able to handle at the moment. Even so minor

*a discomfort as a horse who keeps throwing his head can create frustration in competent riders."*

*"Riding vacations are therefore about finding a guide or wrangler who can listen to what you want, assess what you can accomplish and match you to the horse best suited to your ability. They may not be better riders than you, but they certainly know the horses and their abilities on what may be unfamiliar turf for you. Trust them, and things will start working out very well. They are there to protect you and their horses and the two jobs are definitely related."*

*"Beginners and highly inexperienced riders will find lots of places and opportunities to ride around the world. Your horses will be reliable, sure-footed, bomb-proof, gentle and easy to handle. You are not likely to encounter a situation where you will be ungraciously dumped. Finding good horses for beginners is a relatively easy task for the experienced horse people who operate the vacation destinations. Guest ranches and many pack-supported outfitters have a good stock of horses suitable for those who want to learn. The question of what vacation destination sounds best is answered in the same way as choosing non-adventure oriented travel with one major difference. Riding a horse is a physical activity, even riding one that moves at a walking pace for the duration of your ride. The tension you may bring in to the ride, the position of your legs – which may seem like they are being stretched to eternity, once you dismount – and the movements of the horse are all reasons why you may feel the effects of the ride on your body. Since riding is a physical activity, vacationers want to consider how much time in the saddle will be fun for them and how much recovery time they may need. I think that feeling bone tired from a sporting activity that is fun to do is a great feeling, a medal of honor, if you will, proudly worn and talked about around the camp-fire, the dining room or the lounge. A man must know his limits. Age need not be a concern so long as you are prepared for the after-effects and you have the resources to mount and dismount a horse with or without help."*

*"The point is, don't let your heart be the only factor in choosing*

*a vacation. Consider the needs of your body and you will have one of the most thrilling experiences possible. The exchange between the horse and rider that has fascinated humankind since time immemorial produces a wonderfully fulfilling experience. So mount up – take your family, friend or go by your little old self. Be prepared for the time of your life."*

Mr. Baynard Fox, owner of Equitour, describes his feelings on Equestrian Holidays as follows:

*"I have enough faith in humanity and the course of world events to think that people will continue to turn more and more toward active, mind expanding, adventuresome holidays. There is a growing realization of the mental and physical bankruptcy of sunning on the beach and slipping coins into the slot machines at Las Vegas. People begin to seek more than an aimless, impersonal sightseeing tour by bus. The energetic and intelligent want to have an active, stimulating vacation for mind and body, pursuing*

Baynard and Mel Fox, Owners of Equitours and the Bitterroot Ranch

*a sport they enjoy, meeting new people with whom they have something in common and exposing themselves to new ideas and new ways of doing things."*

*"This kind of holiday is for people who have a strong spirit of adventure and seek new and exciting experiences. It is for those who do not shrink from the occasional dust of the trail, patter of rain on the face or ache of tired muscles and are prepared to break with their old patterns. It is for people who are tired of glass, concrete and traffic and whose hearts leap with joy and exhilaration at the intoxicating freedom of a thundering gallop."*

*"For those with a sense of history and a love of sports there can be no more appropriate way to travel than on horseback. This is how our ancestors, the lucky ones anyhow, used to travel. In parts of Europe and India, the tradition of travel on horseback was never quite lost and many of the old stables, built centuries ago, are being brought into use again. So often, tourism has become a race from one cathedral, waterfall or canyon to another. People are transported by car or plane as quickly as possible from one sight to another. They are almost totally passive and do not participate at all in what is going on unless they are driving themselves and fighting the traffic. This kind of tourism insulates people so effectively from the places they are visiting they might as well be watching their television sets at lesser cost. Riding tours offer travelers more physically and mentally challenging holidays which demand their active participation and bring them into close contact with the people and culture of the places they visit."*

*"On the back of a horse, one is much more part of the country than one can be racing by in a car. Riders are not limited to the roads and see parts of the country most tourists never dream of. They have time to look unhurriedly at the country they traverse and it is easy for them to talk with people along the way. An advantage for real adventures is that people can truly get far from the beaten path."*

*"A typical tour will last one or two weeks and riders will cover twenty to twenty five miles each day, which means five or six hours in the saddle. The price for such a tour runs between one hundred*

to two hundred dollars a day, depending on whether it is a camping trip on the old *Pony Express Trail* or a ride in Kenya. A hotel room in a big city can cost as much and there is no horse, guide or food thrown in. Some rides go at a much faster pace than others and the horses differ in tractability. No rides of this kind are for the complete beginners. Riding is a sport like skiing or mountain climbing which has many degrees of attainment and cannot be safely approached at any level without adequate preparation, but an introduction is easy. The average person of almost any age who is in reasonable physical and mental shape can learn to ride in a week or two of total immersion well enough to handle some of the easier tours. On the other hand, some of the more challenging tours would require several years of experience for most people to handle with safety and enjoyment."

"On the more challenging riding tours, equipment and baggage are usually moved by vehicle so that the riders can move at a varied pace with some trots and some fast gallops. It is less tiring for both people and animals to be able to vary the pace. Ring riding is a good preparation for a riding tour but many beginner riders have gotten a shock when they found how the psychology of the horse and rider can change as they open up on a vast plain in Wyoming or the Hungarian puszta, on a beach in Donegal or running with the zebras in Kenya. It is of vital importance that clients find rides which are appropriate for them so that they are not bored or scared and so that they do not hold up other members of the group."

"No single ride can have everything, but considerations in choosing the best riding tours are the quality of the horses and tack, the food, the wine and the accommodations, the competence, friendliness and knowledge of the guides, the pace of the ride and, above all, the safety. One should also look for such things as historical interest, picturesque culture, architecture, climate, music and other entertainment. It is good to avoid paved roads and noise while seeking remoteness from industrial civilization, contacts with friendly local people and opportunities to view wildlife."

"A great variety of trips are possible in many countries where there is a rich horse culture and there is an abundance of *contrasting opportunities. One can gallop in some of the world's best game areas with giraffe, zebra and wildebeest in Kenya's Out Of Africa Country. One can follow the old Pony Express route or enjoy some of Butch Cassidy's former hideouts in Wyoming. All these places are evocative of folklore and history to educated minds and every bit of it is inextricably entwined with the horses."*

*"The common love of things equinine provides a wonderful entrée everywhere and riders are greeted warmly by local people. A wonderful camaraderie usually forms quickly among the participants. The groups are usually heterogeneous and international, but they all share a fondness for horses. Most riders who travel are enterprising people who are courageous, generous of spirit, well informed, athletic and adventuresome. The stick-in-the-muds, the fearful, the complacent and the narrow-minded will seldom take an Equitour. Many long-term friendships are formed with people one would not otherwise have met. The number of romances which develop is amazingly high."*

*"The aesthetic appeal of riding is enormous. The horse is an animal of such grace, power and beauty that it has fascinated mankind for millennia. Most humans have a very special relationship with horses and it is the partnership between them that made it possible to build civilization. The pleasure of a journey can be greatly enhanced by this partnership with the mount. One has the same feeling of satisfaction in sharing whatever comes with a horse that one can have with a faithful dog."*

*"Horse travel usually has little impact on the environment since horse people seek unsoiled country and tend to be well-attuned to nature. For me, riding day after day on a good horse creates a mood that one could never achieve by modern means of travel."*

*"There are many breeds to choose from around the world. Following are some of the best known in Canada and the United States: The Quarter-horse is the supreme cattle horse, unrivalled for its speed, ability and intelligence.*

*"The Hanoverian horse is the best known of the European warm bloods and an ideal choice for the dressage discipline.*

*"Clydesdale and Percheron horses: both breeds are very tall,*

31

*17h (sixty eight inches) and usually weigh up to two thousand pounds. Both are built for heavy draft work.*

*"Kentucky has the greatest concentration of thoroughbred horse farms in the world around its capital, Lexington.*

*"American standard breeds are used in harness races and also make a fine police horses.*

*"Tennessee walking horses, which evolved in the state of Tennessee, have three gaits: the flat walk, the running walk and the rolling "Rocking Chair" canter, a smooth and collected movement.*

*"The Morgan is a powerful and versatile horse and the first documented American breed.*

*"The Appaloosa is an American spotted breed, developed by the Nez Perce Indians in the mid eighteenth century.*

*"The Palomino, with the striking golden coat and flaxen mane and tail is a color type, rather than a breed.*

*"The Peruvian Paso is noted for its natural, entirely unique lateral gait.*

*"Trakehner, the Trak, is as near as any to being the ideal modern, all-around competition or riding horse.*

*"Andalusian and Lusitano: the Spanish breed is a horse of commanding presence and spectacular paces. The facial profile is convex and the eyes are almond shaped."*

# Chapter 3

# Will Rogers: Shrine of the Sun

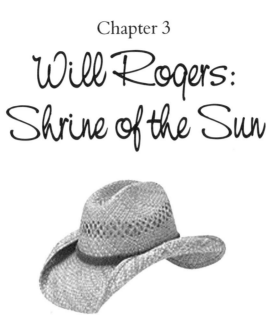

The *Shrine* was built as a memorial to Will Rogers by his friend, Spencer Penrose, founder of the Broadmoor Hotel, and dedicated September 6, 1937. It was designed by the noted architect, Charles E. Thomas. The magnificent edifice is one hundred feet in height above the ground and the base goes down to bedrock, twenty-eight feet below the surface. All the stone in the feudal structure and in the wall around the Garden of Wild Flowers came from one huge boulder quarried nearby. It is estimated that six thousand five hundred cubic yards of stone were used. The altitude here at the Shrine is seven thousand six hundred sixty feet.

The bronze bust of Will Rogers is the work of the distinguished sculptor Jo Davidson. Mr. Davidson has also done the bronze figures of Will which have their place in the Hall of Fame in Washington, D.C. and in the Will Rogers Museum at Claremore, Oklahoma. The chimes at the Shrine ring every quarter of an hour. This is regulated by mechanical control. Floodlights at night throw their silvery beams on the Shrine and it can be seen for miles out on the plains. The site of the Shrine is well chosen. It stands on a promontory that gives command of the vast plains to the east and the mountains to the north, south and west. A beautiful view of Pikes Peak is to be had from this point. In late afternoon, when the sun is setting and the mountain is set in shadow, the Shrine stands out in all its brilliance, bathed in the last rays of the dying day.

Will Rogers loved the wide, sweeping stretches of plains country, which reminded him of the days when he rode the open range. His home near Santa Monica, California had a setting similar to the Shrine, with its mountain background.

In the Shrine are four rooms. Three are devoted entirely to a pictorial review of the life of Will Rogers. The fourth room is known as the historical room and, murals done by Randall Davey, portray the interesting progress of the Pikes Peak region. The pictures in the winding hallway leading up to the Rogers rooms have been carefully selected and are a permanent record of the dedicatory services and other occasions here at the Shrine.

In the Lodge at the entrance to the Shrine gate, there is a guest book wherein there are thousands of names. The Shrine is one of the most unique singing towers in the world. Not only its construction and location, but the man to whom it was dedicated and the pictorial description of his life make this one of the most outstanding structures ever built. As well as chiming out the quarter hours, the Shrine is arranged so that musical concerts can be held over its amplifying system whenever wanted. On clear, windless days, music and chimes from this structure may be heard for distances as great as twenty miles. It took my friend and me over three hours by horseback to climb the seven thousand six hundred sixty feet, to reach the bronze bust of Will Rogers, cowboy and humorist.

The state of Colorado has many interesting sites to visit, including the Garden of the Gods, the Royal Gorge overlooking the Colorado River and many deserted mining towns; all can be reached by flying into Denver and arriving at the new, beautiful airport. From there it is only a sixty-mile drive to Colorado Springs and a few more miles to Manitou Springs.

# Chapter 4

# First Horse Trip Overseas

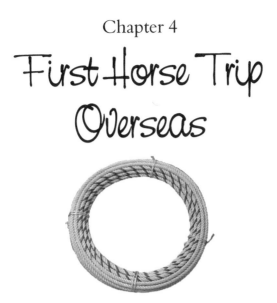

I t was the year 1974, in the month of July, that I took my first overseas horse trip to Hungary. My wife joined the group as a non-rider. While she was pregnant with our first child I was very anxious for her to learn to ride. I finally convinced her to get aboard a usually quiet horse and, as luck would have it, the horse reared its two hind legs, and naturally, my wife slid off. Luckily she wasn't injured physically, but mentally it was a different matter.

I happened to catch a small ad in a horse magazine placed by a woman from Washington who was looking for horse riders to join her for a horse trek through Hungary. The trip included visits to Brussels and Vienna and a hydrofoil along the Danube to Budapest. It looked like a very interesting trip, so leaving our six children, my wife and I went to meet the group at the Westbury Hotel in Brussels. Our hostess, I recall, was a lady in her mid-sixties/seventies, very thin and fragile-looking, but full of energy. The group was almost all American, but one person in particular caught my eye. He was a gentleman of about forty years old, and what made him different was that he had only one arm. The other was just an empty sleeve.

After introductions in this group of twenty people, split evenly between male and female, we traveled to Vienna where we arrived after a four-hour train ride from Brussels.

This was my first time in Vienna, and my wife and I certainly enjoyed the sites, the coffee houses and tasting the various strudels. Of course, we thoroughly enjoyed the few hours we spent at the Spanish Riding School, famous worldwide for the Lipizzaner Stallions.

It takes a full three years to train these stallions. Our guide stated that to get the best of the Lipizzaner, the Vienna school believes in kindness and reward rather than fear of the whip to establish a partnership of horse and rider in order to perform such difficult movements as *Piroette, Passage, Piaffe* and the fabulous *Capriole*, where the horse actually seems to fly as his four legs totally leave the ground simultaneously. This is the most difficult feat. A night at the opera to see *Die Fleidermaus* topped off our two-day stay in Vienna.

Our next new adventure was the hydrofoil ride to Budapest. I didn't realize until I arrived that Budapest is actually two cities, Buda and Pest. We noticed immediately the faces of the citizens, grim and unhappy-looking. They were still under the rule of the communist regime.

From Budapest we left by bus, heading north to the mountain range called the Kekes (3,300 ft.) in the northern province of Nograd, to a village called Vishnagrad. The village is so small that it is not shown on the map of Hungary. It is located near the town of Esztergum, where we stayed in comfortable cabins overnight. We then visited the horses we were to ride at the stables in Vishnagrad and met our guide Tomaz, a very famous ex-cavalryman in the Hungarian army. At the selection, I received a horse called *Gorosh*, a tall, dark bay Gelding. He carried me an average of six to eight hours each day and never let me down.

Being a non-rider, my wife seemed to be enjoying herself riding in the van with the driver, who spoke English and acted as a guide, explaining the sights and pointing out any historical places of interest. The van carried our luggage and lunches and met us

36

at the lunch stops where I was pleased to see my wife assist in the preparation of getting the lunch camp ready. Most lunch meals were on the ground covered with a white tablecloth set with china plates, silverware, and glasses to drink the local Hungarian beer and soft drinks.

I was amazed watching the one-armed American mount and dismount his horse without any assistance; anyone who has never gotten on or off a horse can't imagine how difficult this is using just one arm.

We spent each night in different villages, in hotels, hunting lodges and even in castles. One experience that stands out in my mind after all these years is when arrangements were made by Tomaz and the driver to meet at a certain hour at a particular location. The fun began when Tomaz got completely lost as to his whereabouts, and we were all exhausted when finally, at 8: 00 P.M., we found our driver patiently waiting for us after ten to twelve hours in the saddle. Imagine the stamina of those Hungarian horses holding up after so many hours with riders on their backs.

After six days we arrived at the resort on Lake Balaton, busy with vacationers, families and children. Campers and hotels were situated on the lakefront. After a good night's sleep and a breakfast of bread, jam and coffee, I brought a hand towel down from my washroom to wipe my horse and tack clean before starting off on our last day's ride to explore the sights and sounds around the lake. Upon returning to the hotel to pack, I accidentally threw the hand towel into my carry-on bag. That's a big mistake in a communist-run country, I learned while sitting on the bus waiting to depart. My wife and I and the rest of the group began to get restless after sitting for over an hour. Finally the manager of the hotel appeared at the front door of the bus; through an interpreter he announced that we could not leave until a missing towel was returned. If not, the maid serving our floor would be held responsible with serious consequences to follow. Everyone aboard the bus, including myself, was looking at each other wondering who had stolen the hotel towel.

After fifteen minutes of confusion and discussion, my wife reminded me that perhaps I hadn't returned the small hand towel that she had noticed me using to clean my tack. I immediately confessed that I was the culprit, and I dug deep into my hand luggage and pulled out a dirty, small hand towel. I received an ovation from my fellow riders and finally the bus went on its way to the Budapest airport for our flight home.

Lake Balaton, Hungary trek, July 1974; "Gorush" under saddle

# Chapter 5
# 1981:
# A Super Ride in a Super Country

I t got to be a habit in our family that each year I would take a child alone on a trip so we could spend time together away from the other children. This year it was my only daughter's turn. I purchased a horse and presented it to her on her sixteenth birthday, as she was already an accomplished rider and taking lessons in jumping at the prestigious Eglinton Pony and Hunt Club.

After riding together for many years at the Kingsview Horse Stables, an Irish friend, John McCrae had told me many stories about the stamina and strength of Irish horses. "John," I would say, "I think those Irish horses have more than stamina and strength."

"What do you mean, Hy?"

And I would jokingly reply, "I believe they also have brains, watching you on Bally Shannon after you've drunk your mickey of gin and tilting hard to the right and Bally Shannon shifting her whole body to the right to prevent you from falling!" We both would enjoy a good hardy laugh and then share a drink from his twelve-ounce mickey. Furthermore, I used to watch the Irish army team perform at the Royal Winter Fair each year and most of the time take home the top prizes in all the jumping classes against the tough North American teams in the international horse trials.

I decided to ask my travel agent to inquire about horse treks in Ireland. I had struck gold. She found a gentleman who owned the William J. Riding Stables located in the beautiful Dingle Peninsula. After telling my daughter about horse riding in Ireland, we decided that since this was to be the first time either of us had traveled to Ireland, we might as well tour the island as much as possible in addition to riding.

Upon arriving at the Shannon Airport we rented an auto and with great difficulty, began driving on the left side of the roadways, with the steering wheel on the right side and the gearshift for my left hand. We headed for our first stop, Bunratty Castle.

Bunratty Castle served food as they did five hundred years ago: no forks, knives or spoons. Full and exhausted after a great feast of chicken and more chicken, we took to our rooms for a well-deserved rest.

Our next stop was Tralee, and since this was mid-October, it was cool, damp and rainy. Tralee is located close to the Atlantic Ocean in the southwest of Ireland and very near to our final destination, the Dingle Peninsula, which we planned to explore on horseback. It is actually the west-most point of Europe. In its length of forty-five miles it has a character of its own, combining the grandeur of high mountains, valleys, lakes, forests and many miles of sandy beaches, little coves, islands, cliffs, historic remains, picturesque villages and scattered cottages; in all it is a very spectacular and fascinating area. This is where "Ryan's Daughter" was filmed, starring Robert Mitchum.

I phoned William from Tralee to get final directions to his home, which is only two miles away in a village called Blennerville. There we met three airline stewardesses from Trans World Airlines, which made up the group of five riders. This was to be an eight-day trip. Out of eight days, it rained six.

The owner and our guide was William O'Connor, a fine, good-natured Irishman, who lived quite simply in a five-bedroom home where he would put up his guests for the first night only. His wife cooked and also drove their small vehicle loaded with grain for the horses to each stop on the route. She also prepared our lunches, which always consisted of one apple, one candy bar and one sandwich.

William planned a circular route over seventy-five miles, covering a good portion of Dingle. After selecting the horses, we started via miles of sandy beaches, then crossed to a village named Anascaul and ventured into the valley and mountain trails. Each day brought new vistas, and we galloped on the magnificent four-mile strand through sand dunes.

We rode up to the top of Connor Pass, where we could see Dingle to the south and a panorama of valley, lakes and beaches to the north. We rode into the valley of the cows, which is an inaccessible valley, ringed completely by swooping mountains reachable by horseback.

We spent evenings in quaint rooming houses and hotels where dinner and breakfast were served. I have nothing but praise for the Irish horses. My horse back home would have been crippled after the first day out. It seemed like the Irish horses' legs were made of steel, not bone and flesh.

Goodbye William and onward to Killarney and southeast to Cork to kiss the Blarney Stone. I had always imagined the stone to be a large stone or rock located in a park. I didn't realize it was really on the top floor of a castle approximately three stories high.

Blarney Castle. It is said that those who climb to the top and kiss the stone acquire eloquence. Blarney Castle is situated eight kilometers from the city of Cork and is famous for the stone set into its upper walls. The castle was built in 1146 and was home to several Kings of Munster. The word Blarney is said to have originated with Queen Elizabeth I, who used it to describe "pleasant talk, intended to deceive, without offending."

A full-time gentleman helps to support visitors' backs as they lie down and grip two iron railings, lean backward off the top of the castle, and kiss a block set in its upper walls situated over a gap between the parapet walk and the battlements.

From Blarney we traveled to Waterford and then north towards the foreboding Wicklow mountains. Our route was prepared with reservations at various B&Bs and a final night before Dublin at a fairy-tale castle at Ballymore Eustace.

It was in Ireland that I first tasted the famous Guinness black draft. It took time and then I loved it. Dublin was the last city we visited, and we found the citizens extremely friendly. One night, and then off to New York and on to Toronto.

Second trip overseas with daughter Nadine – 1981

# Chapter 6
## Finally, A Cowboy

Seeing all those western movies each weekend at the matinees during the late 1930's and early 40's, I and probably most of the kids ten to fifteen years of age dreamt of being a cowboy. I watched Hopalong Cassidy, Lone Ranger and Tonto, Tom Mix, Gene Autrey and Roy Rogers and Trigger chasing Indians and riding fast horses and perhaps joining a posse to capture the bad guys.

Ranching, as a daily pursuit, involves one unglamorous, difficult physical task after another: fixing fences, irrigating, repairing equipment, doctoring sick stock, putting up hay, etc. For ranch cowboys, days blend together, and the demands of property and livestock tend to erase words like "weekend," "holiday," and "vacations" from the vocabulary. In spite of the odds against them, ranchers stick with their chosen vocations, fearlessly facing long hours, rough weather and volatile market conditions. I feel fortunate that I was able to realize my fantasies in the cowboy world by actually being there and sharing the lifestyle of a working cowboy.

The cowboy is a mythical character in America. We admire him for his independence, his honesty, his modesty and courage. He represents the best in all Americans as he stares down evil and says, "When you call me that, smile." In fact, these traits were necessary for survival, along with a code of behavior that included loyalty and cooperation. Herding cattle on the vast plains was a lonely, low-paying and dangerous job. Cowboys

had varied backgrounds. Many were blacks, youngsters, former Confederate soldiers and others who found it difficult to get alternative jobs. Their diversity made them appear colorful and romantic to the newspaper writers. However, for a while they were also considered to be hooligans and ruffians. Buffalo Bill's Wild West (and other later Wild West shows) made them popular heroes. The first "King of the Cowboys" was Buck Taylor, a six-foot, six-inch Texan in Buffalo Bill's Wild West. He was a soft-spoken gentleman, but he could also ride, rope, shoot and rescue damsels in distress.

My opportunity to become a cowboy began at the age of fifty-five. It all started on an Air Canada flight in 1982, reading the Air Canada flight magazine "Enroute." In the magazine there appeared an article about guest ranches in Canada and the U.S., giving a descriptive review on what each guest ranch offered, their addresses, phone numbers, etc. One caught my eye immediately; it was called the TX Ranch, an actual working ranch with a thousand head of cattle, run by the Tillett family, located in the Montana-Wyoming border area. At the first opportunity, I called and asked to be mailed a brochure. Here are a few lines from the brochure describing the operation:

Live the West brochure with Hy Burstein featured as a cowboy

*"The TX Ranch is more than a dude ranch; it's an old-fashioned working cattle ranch. Guests help out from mending fences to rounding up and branding cows. Twenty thousand acres straddling the Montana-Wyoming border and another 30 million acres of ranch are leased from*

*the Custer National Forest and Crow reservations located near the Pryor Mountains wild horse range. Abbie Tillett and her four grown children run the operation. Guests sleep in tents and eat home cooked meals prepared over an open fire on a wood-burning cook stove. The TX Ranch offers you the one vacation you'll never forget. Don't just visit the West, Live it!"*

Little did I realize that a few years after I had read their brochure, my photo would appear on their brochure's front page for many years. Living in a large city all my life and then suddenly being thrust onto thousands of acres of open space with no paved roads, traffic or pollution was not only wonderful, but an unforgettable experience.

The adventure began in August 1983, and hasn't stopped yet. I believe I'm their longest-lasting and oldest guest. Many years I would visit the ranch twice each year and stay two weeks instead of the one week they offered.

My two sons, Jay and Dean, both experienced riders, were very anxious to join me on this new adventure. For the first time in our lives we were to become cowboys, real cowboys.

Precisely at 4:00 P.M., two older model Chevrolet Suburbans arrived at the Billings, Montana airport to pick up the guests and their luggage, mostly consisting of duffle bags. Out came one of the drivers and introduced himself as Hip Tillett, son of Abbie Tillett, driver of the Suburban.

Hip had a black eye and what seemed to be a dislocated nose. He was wearing a beat-up dirty felt western black hat. My boys and I sat with Hip on the grueling three-and-a-half-hour drive over some of the roughest cow trails they called a road. This drive gave Hip an opportunity to explain his appearance. A week earlier he had been involved in a bar fight in the town of Lovell, Wyoming, the closest town to his home.

He told us where we were heading: to one of the four cow camps that they use, called the Lone Wolf. The Lone Wolf consisted of one derelict-looking barn, an old rail fence corral and a small broken-down two-story cabin in need of serious repair. There was no running water, no electricity, no plumbing and an outhouse located behind the cabin. The narrow trails had plenty of spider webs and over-grown weeds that could hide snakes. This was a true culture shock. The shack or cabin had one main floor with a coal stove, a table, two benches on either side and a few insulated storage trunks that held our food. This was where we would eat. The family slept upstairs and the guests had small tents to call home.

Hip introduced us to his mother, Abbie, who seemed to be in charge of the place as well as serving as the cook, and his sister Latana, a divorced mother of two. Later in the week I would also meet Hip's dad, whom he called Lloyd. Lloyd was an overweight, proud cattleman who could no longer climb into the saddle although he was only fifty-five. Lloyd had a great sense of humor. He never ran out of stories to tell, all of which had great endings. He was an avid collector of saddles, guns, beer bottles, coins and junk. Lloyd was written up in several books on the history and beginnings of the early settlers in Montana. Hip had a brother called Will, who ran off to New Zealand. Will's right arm was shot off by Hip in a hunting accident when they were in

John McRae and Hy

their early-teens. His sister Gail helped in the small kitchen and another sister, Laina, was married and living in Alaska.

From 1983 to the 1990's, I visited the ranch twice yearly and began to learn a great deal about the Tillets. They certainly were an interesting family. Lloyd originally came from Texas and was one of the earlier settlers in Montana. He married Abbie who was a descendent of the Crow Indian tribe. Together they raised five children. Will was the eldest and the most favored by Lloyd. Hip was the youngest. Latana was the best horseman of the three girls, working the cattle and an outstanding rider. The other two girls would help Abbie when guests arrived. The cattle operation that they ran together with Lloyd's brother Royce wasn't profitable. Their next-door neighbor Joe Bassett started to accept guests at his ranch called Schively and so did Lloyd and his two sons in 1980.

Comparing the two ranches is like comparing a Cadillac to a Volkswagen. Whereas the Schively Ranch supplied cabins beds, electricity and facilities for showers, the Tilletts gave guests at that time just a small tent, a plastic ground sheet and no electricity, which meant no telephone, no radio, no power of any kind. They

Tepees idea lasted two years only - wind knocks them over

were really back to the basics. Perhaps that was the attraction of the Tilletts – to go back to the living style of a hundred years ago.

The first few years I spent visiting the Tilletts, I had never met Hip's brother Will. Rumor had it that Will was wanted by the sheriff's office of Lovell, Wyoming for some minor infraction of the law. He refused to be questioned about it and so left for Australia and New Zealand. There he met an attractive young lady who became his wife. When the legal problems were resolved, Will returned home. Will, his wife Nickie, and their two children returned to the United States and became involved with the guest part of the operation.

One of the ideas that Will wanted the family to try was to change the sleeping quarters for the guests from tents to tepees, which they did in 1993. This idea lasted only two seasons, as the wind in Montana in the spring and autumn is unrelenting, and the guests did not appreciate the rain entering the tepee from the top where all the long wooden poles came together, resulting in soaked blankets and sleeping bags.

In the mid 1980's I met a Dr. and Mrs. See from Tennessee and their daughter and son-in-law as guests of the TX. Dr. See was a fine old gentleman, and, in fact, he gave me advice that I have passed on to many others. It seemed that each night I would have to rise from the warm comfort of my sleeping bag, zip open my tent and step outside in the cool weather to relieve myself at least three or more times, and again another three or more times in the morning after breakfast. Dr. See from Tennessee told me not to drink coffee and that would cause me to urinate less frequently. His suggestion worked. Just plain common sense. His son-in-law, who was an excellent cowboy and an expert at roping, shocked Hip and me at the Deadman Camp on his day of departure back to Tennessee. He asked Hip for help in removing his high western boots. His right boot came off nicely, but when he went to pull his left boot, his artificial leg from his thigh came along with his boot. Evidently he released his artificial leg on purpose to get the shock effect and it worked. On watching this cowboy get on and off his horse, you would never tell he had an artificial leg.

I can report that the Tillett family ranch now uses large heavy-duty canvas tents, each supplied with a wood-burning stove, and spring beds eighteen inches off the ground for use with a sleeping bag. Cooking is now done on propane stoves, which replaced the small wood stove that Abbie used; of course, outhouses are still used, while Schively Ranch has flush toilets and hot and cold running water. Schively uses a generator to keep their food fresh in a large walk-in container, whereas the Tillets keep their supplies in small, insulated boxes. Beer is still kept cold by placing the can or bottle in a cold running creek passing through their campsite. That's been the attraction for many loyal Tillet ranch guests who keep returning every year, perhaps reminding them of what their ancestors had to endure and maybe to appreciate what they have in their modern way of life and perhaps not to take even the flick of a light switch for granted.

The drive from Billings to the TX Ranch "Deadman" Camp takes approximately three to four hours, all depending on the weather. The last town we reach before heading north into Montana State is Lowell, Wyoming. This is the last chance to purchase fuel, food, beverages and supplies. An hour out of Lovell brings us to the Big Horn Canyon, not as well known as the Grand Canyon, but just as impressive. The canyon's height is approximately five hundred feet and at the bottom runs a winding river for sixty miles that in summer is used for boating.

As we proceed to "Deadman" we pass the wild horse range, where many mustangs can be seen grazing and, with a sharp lookout, we can see many big horn sheep and rams climbing up and down steep stone ledges. Once we reach "Deadman," surrounded by red-colored cliffs, we now understand why they call Montana "land of the big sky." What a pleasure – no traffic, no high-rise buildings and no noise. The Indians had it all.

The road leading to Abbie and Lloyd's home is a winding, dusty, remote country mountain pathway a dozen miles or so from any store or neighbor except for Lloyd's brother Royce, whose home you pass on the way to Lloyd's. Royce was a partner in the cattle operation only; Royce did all the irrigation and haying, while Lloyd was in the cattle end. Everything ran smoothly until Royce died in the mid 1990's, and then the great family feud began. After years of litigation and costly lawyers' fees, an agreement was finally reached where Hip and Abbie took over the complete operation: the cattle, irrigation and haying.

Over the many years I have spent at the TX, I have met people from many parts of the U.S.A., as well as many overseas guests from Belgium, Germany, England, Japan and Australia, among others. Today, the TX is run solely by Hip, his wife Loretta and their two daughters, Desiree and Shaina. His brother Will has since divorced his wife Nickie and is remarried and lives in Lowell, Wyoming. His sister Gail has married and sister Latana, once his right-hand wrangler, has now retired, looking after her children. Sadly, Hip's sister Laina and his dad Lloyd have both passed away.

Even though Hip's brother Will had the use of only one arm, he could saddle-up and mount without anyone's assistance and could ride the toughest horses. In fact, I remember bringing Will

TX Ranch – Hy, Rags, Will Tillet

Schively Ranch – Hy with Son, Mory

a wristwatch as a gift and he didn't have it on for five minutes when he broke it riding a bucking bronco. As far as Hip's riding ability, it was just awesome. He could gallop full speed down the steepest slopes and chase cows and steers from hiding places that were dangerous for horses to reach. His roping skills, whether on the ground or chasing a calf on horseback, were a pleasure to watch. He was truly a cowboy's cowboy.

In late October of 2000, fearing an early winter, Hip closed his guest operation and would not take on any reservations. Since my only opportunity to go west that year was in early November, I decided to visit the arch-enemy of the TX ranch, the Schively Ranch, run by Joe Basset and his family. The Schively Ranch happens to adjoin the TX, and these neighbors have never gotten along. There has been an ongoing feud between them for many years. As it happened, there was no early winter. In fact, the weather was mild. I felt guilty and a traitor staying at the Schively until I thought, I could act as a spy for Hip and report about Joe Basset's operation.

There wasn't one derogatory fault I could find in Joe, his wonderful wife and their children. They were gracious hosts.

51

However, since they were Mormons, we weren't allowed any alcoholic beverages and saying grace before our meals was new to me. In my opinion, they ran a terrific operation and so thought my son Mory and his friend Jay.

Back in 1991, while awaiting our pick-up at the Billings airport, my son Mory and I noticed an extremely well-dressed and handsome dude and his attractive wife. What made them noticeable was the designer clothes they were both wearing, especially his exotic-skin western boots. I could not imagine that this couple was going to the TX Ranch. I introduced myself and after a few minutes, learned that Mr. Ken Rubinstein and his wife Amie were from Long Island, N.Y. and both enjoyed riding horses. Looking for a dude ranch to visit, they found the majority sold-out because of the publicity from the movie "City Slickers," starring Billy Crystal and Jack Palance. The only available ranch was the TX. After spending the week together at the ranch, Ken, his wife, my son Mory and I became good friends. It was just unfortunate that Amie received a kick to her leg just below the knee on her first day out and was sidelined the rest of the week. Ken and Amie came to Mory's wedding in Toronto and also to his twin brother Dean's wedding a few years later. My wife and I had the good fortune to visit the Rubinstein's estate on Long Island and meet their three children. Ken returned to the TX for

Cattle drive – TX Ranch

Cattle Drive – 1985

two more trips with me, but both proved to be disastrous.

On the first trip, a guest from Germany was a Nazi-type who blamed the Jews for starting World Wars I and II. Being a lawyer and Jewish, Ken was constantly arguing with this Nazi-type and this naturally spoiled his vacation. I have learned over the years that on holidays you don't discuss politics or religion.

When I called Ken to join me again for another adventure to the TX, I assured him that there would be no further Nazi-type guests and suggested that perhaps he should bring his son this time. Ken agreed and brought his twenty-year-old son, and I also brought my son. We met a night before in Billings.

Now, since Ken enjoyed his comfort, he and I decided to rent our own vehicles. Ken wanted the freedom of leaving the ranch any time he chose. So off went Ken to a large outdoor fitter store, where he purchased his own tent, lanterns, flashlight, thick foam pads to place under the sleeping bags for comfortable sleeping and all sorts of other supplies.

Our caravan consisted of the TX beat up Chevrolet Suburban with my four-wheel-drive S.U.V. and Ken's vehicle behind us. This time our campsite would be "Hank's Place," which is located in a picture-postcard setting, but to get there we had to drive through grazing land and dirt trails, climb up rocky slopes, and down into ravines. In dry weather it's quite hazardous, but as luck would have it, rain started as soon as we left Billings. As we left the highway to enter the reservation land it was already dark and the heavy downpour caused the vehicles to slip and slide, and slide they did. Ken's vehicle, with Ken behind the wheel, slid right into an embankment, and he stopped when his vehicle tilted to such a degree that it looked as if it would flip over on its side.

In my rearview mirror I saw that he was falling behind, so I blinked my headlights so that the TX Surburban would also stop. After an agonizing forty-five minutes in the heavy downpour with Ken refusing to sit behind the wheel for fear that his car might roll on its side down the embankment, we all pushed and lifted, with mud flying in all directions, getting us all wet and covered in mud. We arrived at the campsite after 9:00 P.M., and thank goodness, all the tents were up. However, Ken refused to sleep in the tent allotted to him and decided he and his son

Nadine, The Great Cattle Drive – 2002

At work

would erect the tent they had purchased in Billings, which was supposedly waterproof.

The rain did not subside and, in fact, came down even harder. After struggling for another hour, soaked to the skin, the pair finally got to rest. After the third day of riding, Ken decided, over the objections of his son, to leave and return to New York to the comfort of his own home.

The second gentleman that I had enjoyed meeting and riding with for several years was Ben Ragsdale – Rags for short. A very courageous rider, I thought, watching him ride so fearlessly, until I discovered that he was an alcoholic and was constantly drinking from early morning to evening.

In fact, since his favorite drink was called "Bushmill," a great tasting scotch, when he purchased a steer from Hip he named the steer "Bushmill." He went as far as registering his own branding iron that he designed and had the thrill of branding his own cow. Eventually the steer put on weight and was sold at a profit.

Ben lived in Memphis, Tennessee and had a super personality. I visited Rags in Memphis in 1990. He was a very gracious host, and we spent time touring the city sights, including Graceland,

Elvis Presley's mansion, and his private bus and plane. Rags has since married and given up alcohol and, therefore, given up riding and no longer visits the TX. The last year I saw Rags at the TX was in 1992. I have talked to him on numerous occasions and he now has three children and works with his wife making artwork for Hollywood, advertising new movies being released.

After visiting the TX Ranch for many years, one evening I was sitting with some guests around the campfire when, for the first time, I heard Hip make a racist remark: "I don't like the French people or Jews!" I was a bit shocked, and then I realized he didn't know that I was Jewish.

The next morning I confronted Hip and asked him why he didn't like Jews, as I had met many of his Jewish guests other than Ken and Amie and all seemed quite nice and friendly.

"They talk too loud and can be very noisy," was his reply.

"Noisy?" I asked, "I've met dozens of your guest who, after their drinking binges, would keep me up all night with their

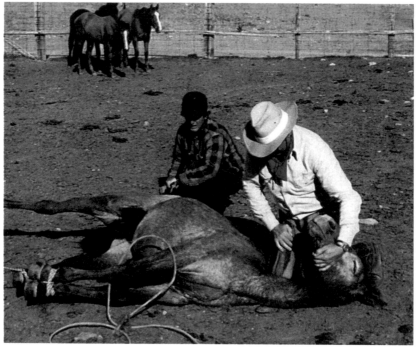

Holding head to avoid injury

Distributing salt blocks for cattle at TX Ranch with team of donkeys

loud voices, and believe me, they weren't Jewish. Besides, I'm Jewish."

"What? You can't be, and if you are, you're different," he replied in disbelief, and his face turned a deep red.

"Hip, I may not be religious, and I lean toward atheism, but I was born to Jewish parents and that makes me a Jew."

I received and accepted his apology, and then his final words, "Those Israelis sure know how to fight a war."

Over the past nineteen years at the TX, I have participated in all forms of cattle ranching, including branding, dehorning (which means clipping the horns off) – a very painful process for the steer – castrating, ear tagging, pregnancy testing, loading and unloading the cows, and cattle drives in the freezing cold weather as well as in the heat. I once attempted to ride a steer after he was just branded and was thrown very hard, landing on my back. I actually saw stars. Branding horses is different. A older horse can be branded quickly and easily by just putting a cover over his head. A colt or filly is a different matter, and truthfully, I didn't enjoy what Hip had instructed. I and a few other guests had to rope the horse around the neck and pull his neck so hard in order to cut his breathing ability until he dropped to the ground so that Hip could tie up his legs, and then I had to hold his head on my lap so that the horse wouldn't injure himself. After the branding, he was released.

All of my five sons have visited the TX at some time and even have returned more than a few times. The city of Billings is only thirty miles from Custer National Park, where General Custer lost his life with two hundred of his fellow officers and men at Little Big Horn Battleground fighting perhaps up to five thousand Indians. At the site, a stone monument was placed where each soldier fell with the soldier's name written on a plaque. The

Chief Plenty Coup

tourist office also offers a film depicting the famous battle, and all types of souvenirs and pictures can be purchased.

A visitor to the Billings area can take a short drive to Red Lodge, a skiing community with a large statue of the famous Indian Chief Plenty Coup to greet you as you enter this pleasant town. Plenty Coup was famous for negotiating peace for his

Irma Hotel built by Buffalo Bill Cody – Cody, Wyoming

Overlooking Buffalo Bill Museum
Cody, WY

own tribe, Crow, with the Union Army and helped them in their cause against the Sioux Nation and Blackfoot tribes. There is a refurbished historical hotel and a few interesting restaurants and shops.

Last, but not least, is Cody, Wyoming – the gateway city to Yellowstone – named after Buffalo Bill Cody, who founded the city at the turn of the century and constructed a hotel named after his daughter Irma, at the cost of eighty thousand dollars. The hotel was soon embellished with a one hundred thousand dollar cherrywood bar. This magnificent artifact was made in France and shipped to the east coast, then carried by rail to Red Lodge, Montana and finally by wagon to Cody. For years it has been the second most photographed item in Cody, second only to the Scout Statue of Buffalo Bill at the end of Cody's main street. The bar was a gift from Queen Victoria in appreciation for the

At the "Lone Wolf" camp in Montana

59

great Wild West Show that Buffalo Bill Cody produced with an American cast in Great Britain. Cody built this fine hotel for housing and enter-taining important guests, including politicians and government officials.

Cody's main street has some great shopping for western clothes, artifacts and western art by some of the best western artists, including John Clymer, Fredric Remington and Charles Russell.

To get into the western mode without horses, there is the western dance club, Cassidy's, where I met Henry Winkler (the Fonz) right there on the dance floor.

I spent a full day going back into history by visiting the Buffalo Bill Museum. It took me back to the times when the Indians and buffalo roamed the plains of Wyoming and Montana. It also features a large section about William Cody's life from the time of his youth right to the end of his career. There is also a model room containing the original clothes he wore, tables, desks and chairs he used, his private collection of pistols and rifles, and bronze statues and paintings.

## Chapter 7

# Spain with Nadine

I found an interesting ad in the newspaper with the words,
"Spain on Horseback" in large block letters, which sparked
my interest. My daughter Nadine mentioned that she was
offered a modeling job in Barcelona, Spain, in early May, 1984.
Since she was an experienced rider, I thought this was a good
opportunity for us to meet. I made my connections with the
owner of Rutas Cabello, Mr. Antonio Alcantera. He told me
about a ride for eight days in the latter part of May. This worked
out quite well with my daughter's timetable. This was my first
trip ever to Spain, and since Nadine had already been in Barcelona
for three weeks, she knew her way around and was very excited
to act as my tour guide.

She first took me to Las Ramblas Street, Barcelona's famous
pedestrian walkway, with autos running north and south on
either side. The center boulevard is cluttered with kiosks selling
goods of every description, small cafes and shoeshine stands.
At the south end, which ends at the sea, stands a breathtaking
monument to Christopher Columbus, Spain's most famous
voyager, rising to a height of fifty meters. The structure cuts a
dramatic pose against the skyline, as the great explorer gazes out
to sea, documents in hand, gesturing toward some faraway spot
located well beyond the horizon.

First trip to Spain with Nadine – 1984

Spain with Nadine

Built in the nineteenth century to commemorate Columbus's return from his first trip to the Americas, the statue has become a favorite landmark for natives and tourists alike, but for all its popularity, an air of mystery surrounds the site. Rather than depicting Columbus pointing westward, in the direction of the Americas he is credited with discovering, it portrays him facing east, as if being pulled in the direction of the Holy Land.

The south end of Las Ramblas is also the old section of Barcelona, featuring prostitutes, pimps and seedy characters; it also has the best paella you can find in Spain. This area also features the best bargains in ladies shoes, handbags and luggage.

After a short flight back to Madrid, the taxi took us to the hotel that Rutas Cabello chose for our overnight stay and picked us up the following morning. After breakfast, we met our fellow guests and off we went to Segovia, Spain and dinner at the Candido Restaurant. Segovia features one of the largest and highest aqueducts that the Romans built in the occupation of Spain. This aqueduct runs right through the city of Segovia, and the autos and trucks still drive between the columns that support them. After a two-hour drive from Segovia, we came to the starting point of our ride, "The Mill" at Molino De Rio Viejo, where Mr. Antonio Alcantera owns a lovely two-story home capable of sleeping eighteen guests comfortably, and featuring a huge kitchen and lovely stone fireplace in the dining room, which after dinner becomes the living room.

The next morning right after the selection of the horses, which were stabled next to the home, we were able to move quickly since there were only five guests. During this seven-night journey we stayed overnight in Paradors and comfortable hotels. The Santa Maria De El Paular was our main riding center in this marvelous monastery hotel. Spanish wine was served at every lunch and dinner.

"Get to know Spain from the Saddle" was the slogan that really illustrates the reality of traveling on horseback. We traveled through the marvelous infrastructure of ancient sheep trails, cattle tracks, wagon bridle paths and the thousands of intertwining paths of Spain. The ride was a great adventure, but little did I know that a greater adventure would unfold very soon after the conclusion of our ride. Nadine and I said farewell to Antonio and then returned to Barcelona.

It all started when Nadine and I left Barcelona via an automobile that I had rented, and headed east in the direction of Italy. At this point, I knew that a young man by the name of Bruce had dated Nadine a few times, but didn't realize to what extent he cared for her. Upon arriving in Rome and checking into a prearranged hotel in central Rome, my daughter confessed that she had talked to Bruce and mentioned to him our traveling schedule and names of hotels. Sure enough, there were telephone messages left for her, and I heard that there was a possibility of him coming to Rome. I had no intention of Bruce coming between my daughter and me and spoiling our vacation, so I decided to pack up and leave one day earlier. We had already visited all the most important sites, including the Vatican, the various piazzas, fountains, the Coliseum, the Spanish Steps, etc.

As we were loading the car to leave for the Rome airport, not only did Bruce show up, but his sister Caryn was with him. They both tried to convince Nadine to stay in Rome. After all, they had

just arrived and didn't think it fair for us to leave. They offered her a further tour of Rome, dinner and better hotel accommodations if perhaps she would stay over a few more nights and suggested that I continue with my travel plans to Israel alone, and Nadine would follow. I told my daughter it was up to her, she could do as she pleased. My daughter looked at me, felt I was upset, and told Bruce politely that she was going to leave with me.

I felt relieved by her decision, and off we went to catch our flight to Tel Aviv. From Ben Gurion Airport the taxi delivered us to the Tel Aviv Hilton. The following morning, at breakfast, there he was again, enjoying his fresh-squeezed orange juice with a grin from ear to ear. Bruce won the battle of Nadine's heart with his display of determination and persistence. He also won his battle with me. In less than a  year they were married.

Chapter 8

# Another Visit to Spain

My second venture to Spain was in the month of June, 1986, and my advice to anyone contemplating a horse trip to Spain would be to avoid May, June or July. Temperatures in these months can hover between ninety and one hundred degrees Fahrenheit. During this particular ride my riding companion was the elder of my twin sons, Mory. Our meeting place was the colorful city of Seville, where we were to meet up with our guide, Antonio, the owner of Rutas Cabellos and a prominent lawyer from Madrid, and his daughter Elian. Antonio's other daughter, Estelle, ran the kitchen and restaurant at "The Mill" at Molino de Rio Viejo. Our other riding companions were three young women who lived outside of Seville and one American female rider.

Our starting point this time was in El Cortido De El Santiscal, located in the picturesque town of Arcos De La Frontiera in the province of Cadiz. This is a second home and stable that Antonio uses for his guests and includes a good-sized swimming pool. My son and I went into town the first evening and found it lively with music, food stands, carnival games and people generally enjoying themselves in a well-lit atmosphere.

On the horse selection, I was given a typical Spanish breed, a part Andalusian white stallion named Bandito. Our trail took us on a southern route through the province of Seville, Cadiz y Malaga. We enjoyed fresh salads each day with oil and salt dressings, and nothing tasted as refreshing on a hot day like the cold bowls of gazpacho soup at the tavernas that we stopped at each day. We sampled the tapas, red wine and cold beer after the horses were unsaddled.

After six days, the ride ended on the beach of Cadiz, which is on the Atlantic Ocean. It's a stop for many cruise ships that enter or leave the Mediterranean Sea. After we bid farewell to Antonio and his daughter, their van returned us to Seville, where we acquired a car and began touring Spain. We visited Cordoba, the home of Maimonides, b1135-d1204 – philosopher, rabbi and physician, and also called the Rambam.

From Cordoba we headed south to Granada, where we found pleasant accommodations. The next morning we set out for Alhambra outside of Granada, which was the palace of the Moorish Kings. It was built during the thirteenth and fourteenth centuries. It seems that the kings and nobles had a great time there with many harems, judging from the amount of sleeping and bedrooms quarters built for them. After a few hours of touring Alhambra, off we went to the south coast of Spain, to Malaga.

Driving east of Malaga along the Costa del Sol we passed through fabulous resort areas. They are truly the playgrounds of the rich. These rich folks are tourists mainly from Germany and Great Britain. We continued on to Algeciras, where we purchased a ferry ticket thinking it was for the trip across the Strait of Gibraltar to Morocco. However, when we disembarked, I thought everything looked so clean and orderly. Little did I know we were actually still in Spain. I never realized that Spain had a small foothold on the African continent by the name of Ceuta, which is a small city sitting on the tip of the northern-most point of Morocco.

Synagoga – Cordoba, Spain

Mory and Maimonides – Cordoba, Spain

After getting some directions, we headed in our rental car for the border crossing to Morocco. That was an experience in itself, with the crowds of Moroccans lined up to return and the chaos at the passport control office. Not speaking or reading Arabic or Spanish, I had no idea what to do or where to turn for help crossing the frontier with hundred of people in cars, walking, pushing and crowding the one and only entrance to passport control. Most of the Moroccans were dressed in long robes and sandals and it all looked so strange to my son and me. We were about to return to mainland Spain when a young chap, who must have noticed our difficulty, offered to help us for fifteen dollars. He took both of our passports and returned one hour later with our passes.

Once in Morocco and on our way to Rabat, I realized that the delay at customs was worth it. Rabat is the capital of Morocco, where the king's palace is situated. Our aim now was to get to Casablanca, which was approximately one hundred miles to the south along the coastline of the North Atlantic Ocean. We had heard there was a Hyatt hotel where we could have a decent meal and a good night's rest.

Entrance to Fantasia – Marrakech, Morocco

Entrance to Fantasia – Marrakech, Morocco

Water Boy – Downtown Marrakech

The following day we hired a professional guide and toured this interesting and very cosmopolitan city. We saw no sign of Humphrey Bogart or Ingrid Bergman-types or the Casbah. Two hundred miles to the south was the fabulous city of Marrakech in a spectacular setting at the base of a snowcapped Atlas mountain. This is the beginning of Berber territory. The land is still much as it was before the Arab invasion. There are high desert plateaus and lush valleys to traverse.

The city of Marrakech is the most interesting and colorful I have visited throughout the world. It is a city of many contrasts. For example, my son and I took a room at the Mamuma Hotel, the most luxurious hotel in western Africa, or perhaps all of Africa. Then there's the famous city square, which is not a square, but an enormous circular area, filled with magicians, snake charmers, sword swallowers and watermen in their colorful red costumes selling fresh water. We also saw tooth-pullers, trained monkeys, acrobats and hundreds of small food kiosks offering a variety of sweets, meats, dairy products, herbal medicines and herbs of all types. The activities continued on until late evening, as more and more people arrived to join the festivities.

The greatest surprise was in the evening as we visited the extravaganza called Fantasia. We arrived for a pick-up at our hotel to drop us at the front gates of the Fantasia club. As we passed through the gates, we found ourselves walking along a red carpet until we arrived at an honor guard of twenty-five or more. Berber horsemen were dressed in Arab costume and mounted on superb horses that later performed and demonstrated their riding skills in an outdoor arena the size of Madison Square Garden. As we entered we were met by a hostess who led us to our private table. On the way, we found musicians lined on both sides playing their different instruments. Belly dancers, fire eaters, a galaxy of singers and drummers were all trying to entertain us on our long walk to a most beautifully designed tent that made us feel like kings. The scantily dressed young ladies were eager to serve us the most scrumptious meal. Mory and I felt disappointed to leave this wondrous small city of Marrakech.

71

Our last stop was the historic city of Fez with its famous Medina. We were both concerned when two motorcycles started to follow our auto from about twenty miles outside of Fez, and kept pulling up alongside wanting us to stop and also shouting offers of drugs to sell us. We could not shake these characters even with threats that I would contact the police. They followed us right to the front entrance of the five-star hotel. Finally, the doorman told them to disappear. We immediately hired a guide and took off for the Medina, which is the old native quarter of a North African city and crowded with throngs of people shopping for merchandise of every description. Our guide led us into a large carpet store where my son and I were hassled for over an hour or more to purchase their rugs. They would not let us leave and for a while, I felt concerned for our safety. The guide disappeared, and there were huge piles of rugs and carpets. I had difficulty finding my way out.

Back out in the open we had at least a dozen offers to sell us hashish or any drugs we wanted. We refused all offers to buy or become carriers. This turned out to be a wise decision as our auto was the first in line to board the ferry back to Spain. When the ferry docked, we were first off the ship and immediately were stopped by Spanish police with their sniffer dogs and ordered out of our vehicle. We watched as they literally tore the rental apart. They found nothing and let us go on our way. It was a good lesson for future travels. Don't get involved with anyone asking you to do them a favor by carrying any drugs or packages. On our arrival to mainland Europe, it seemed as though we had just left a different planet.

Our destination was now Lisbon, to get our flight back to North America. We saw the outline of the Rock of Gibraltar and traveled north up the coastline of Spain passing Cadiz and onward across to Portugal, stopping overnight in a town called Faro. Little did I realize then that within ten years I would be riding horses in this area with a group of American riders. This ended my second trip to Spain.

# Chapter 9

# Spain
# For the Third Time

T his third trip was completely different from the past two. I was so impressed with Spain that I decided to accept Antonio's invitation for a thirty-day ride starting in Segovia and traveling straight south almost through the center of Spain down to Cadiz, following an old cattle drive route called the Cānāda. In some areas the trail can be twenty feet wide and in others a few hundred feet wide. This trip took place in the month of October, which meant pleasant weather.

Again I was told to meet in Madrid, where the pick-up was to be made. It was in the hotel that I discovered five U.S. gentlemen were also going to join in the thirty-day ride. The five men were all friends from the San Francisco area and included Mr. Mody Sabran, Mr. Tom Smith, a judge, Mr. Joe Geller, a lawyer, Dr. Jay Smith, a physician and Mr. Grant Banion, retired and the oldest of the group at seventy. It so happens that I have kept up a close relationship with these gentlemen and have traveled to California many times to ride with them. We also have traveled to many countries for horse treks. Their favorite drink was bourbon while mine was vodka.

As on the first ride, we made our selection of horses at "The Mill" at Molino De Rio Viejo. It was here that we met two other

Third time thirty day ride – Spain

guests who were to join us. There was a quiet chap from England and a mouthy lady from Germany who, after dinner on our first evening at "The Mill," started to talk about the supremacy of the German people and about how the Americans were inferior soldiers to the German army. Wow, that's all the American riders had to hear!

I selected *Brilliante*, a superb horse, and I knew that if he was to carry me for thirty days I would have to ride off his back to prevent any back problems, which simply means to ride as jockeys do, out of the saddle.

Off we went with overweight Antonio in the lead, heading for our first night stop at the walled city of Avila De Los Caballeros, the best-preserved wall in any European city. We did quite a bit of galloping that first day, and two horses were already lame and could not continue. Antonio declared that from now on he would have to take it at a slower pace, so as not to have any further problems, as he had only four or five spare horses.

The next morning we had two new riders. One was an American gentleman from Key Largo, who ran an underwater hotel especially for honeymoon couples called the Jules Undersea

Lodge, the world's first and only underwater hotel. The other was an American woman who fell off her horse on the first day and broke her ankle. This forced her to cancel the remainder of her ride. They both arrived late because of poor flight connections.

One hundred miles and four days later we reached the birthplace of Francisco Pizzaro, the Spanish conqueror of Peru, in the city of Trujilo. In the thirteenth and fourteenth centuries Trujilo had been a city of learning, and approximately five thousand Jews lived and studied there. They also worshipped in the few synagogues that have since been converted to churches. Mr. Joe Geller had with him a guidebook that mentioned a street with the address of a pharmacy that had at one time been a small school for Jewish learning. Joe and I took a walk and found the pharmacy. We asked the person behind the counter if this store had any historical significance. He pointed to an archway entrance to a lower floor. Over the archway were fading Hebrew letters, which I copied as best I could, and sure enough, the letters spelled out "school for children, school for learning."

During the first five or six days riding none of the men in the group spoke to the German rider, whose name was Hilda Brandt. They completely ignored her during breakfast, lunch and dinner.

As we were riding in the southern direction, we thought it would get warmer, but no, it was getting cooler, and the light leather jacket I was wearing was not much help. In fact, Antonio was himself surprised and said that he had never felt so cold this time of year. We passed through many villages and forests, crossed streams, rode deep canyons and could spot many vultures flying overhead. Along the trails there were many gates to open, and Dr. Jay Smith was always the first to reach the gates and dismount and say the same line each time: "Dismounting is like having a refreshing cup of coffee." Many a time we arrived at a fence, found no gate and were forced to use wire cutters to get through.

From Trujilo we swung to the east to reach Guadalupe and visited the famed monastery. After giving the horses a well-deserved rest for a few hours, we started in a southerly direction again, headed for the province of Cordoba. We were now close to the halfway point of our trek and were nearing Seville.

After riding now for sixteen days, we were looking forward to a two-day rest in Seville and were anxious to see the Flamenco dancers in action. After the first day of rest, Mr. Antonio Armero Alcantera called for a meeting in our hotel located in the old section of Seville. The meeting proved to be a shocker. Antonio told us we could no longer ride south; there was a quarantine called by the government of all horses south of Seville. If we had continued riding, the horses would have been seized and put into quarantine for possibly two or more months. He had already phoned his office to send down trucks to pick up the horses and transport them back to the mill.

However, he gave us two choices to think about. The first choice was that he would take whoever was interested on a motorized tour of the region or we could ride our horses back to the mill at a quicker pace. At the guest meeting there were nine of us to decide. Dr. Jay Smith, the judge, and I decided to ride the horses back to the mill. The Englishman and the German woman wanted to return immediately to their homelands and the four remaining Americans chose to tour.

We were all saddened at this turn of events and unhappy that we had to split up. At dinner we said our goodbyes and then I realized that since I was going north again, I would require either a sweater or a jacket. I chose a down-filled jacket to keep me warm through the wind and rain that we faced heading back.

Our guide and the three of us made fairly good time with only two stops for lunch and what they called pit stops. Our routine was to walk for a half-hour, trot for fifteen to twenty minutes, gallop for five minutes and back again for that half-hour walk. None of the four horses became lame and their backs were not sore. We finally reached the mill and looked forward to a hot meal and a good night's rest.

Antonio mentioned that when we got back to Madrid he would like to have Jay, Tom and me over for dinner at his apartment to meet his wife before we left Madrid. He suggested we stay at an airport hotel. Antonio arranged to have us picked up and we arrived at his residence where we met his charming wife and discussed Spanish politics, Spanish horses, Spanish bullfights and Spanish Toreadors. Over some full-flavored Spanish wine we told Antonio that the most interesting part of the trek was visiting two ranches where bulls are raised and bred for fighting and we enjoyed watching the young men learning the ropes of bull fighting, hoping perhaps to become as famous as American baseball players. I must point out that this training takes place in a much smaller bullring when they practice and that it can be dangerous.

After a few nightcaps, Jay, Tom and I said our farewells to our hosts and then took a taxi to our airport hotel. It was certainly a disappointment that we did not complete our thirty-day horse trek as planned. However, our group can be thankful that none of us got injured or required medical attention. Anyway, it was back to Toronto and viva la Espania.

Big Red – 1985

## Chapter 10

# Fox Hunting

A hunting we will go... In 1985 I joined a colleague of mine on a hunt in the beautiful Halton Hills, bringing my horse Big Red, whom I had obtained just six months before. Big Red was part of a two-horse team and had never had a saddle on his back. In other words, he never had a rider on his back either. I learned that the hard way when I first brought him to my farm after purchasing him from my old friend Al Greco of the Circle M Ranch. I wasn't on his back one minute when Big Red reared straight up on his hind legs, lost his balance and flipped over backwards with me still in the stirrups. I could have been seriously injured, but fortunately it was muddy and soft where we landed – me on the bottom, Big Red on the top. When we both got up, I could see the outline of my back in the mud. We all called him "tank" due to his weight of over thirteen hundred pounds and his lack of manners, swiping at any horse that dared to cross his path.

Actually, I loved Big Red. I loved his smooth gait at the trot and canter. I called him the Cadillac of horses. It was always a challenge for me to ride him as he was full of surprises at all times, and as large as he was, he acted many times like a frightened child.

I eventually joined the Innisclare Hunt Club and brought two of my sons as riding guests on every hunt. They would help me load the horse, tack and hay. Since the hunts started at 8:00 A.M. each Sunday in the fall, it meant rising at 6:00 A.M. to get the horses groomed, loaded and driven to the various starting points. This period lasted for two years, and it was another learning experience for me, my two sons, Mory and Dean, and of course, Big Red.

Our hunts usually took two to three hours, starting with one rider dragging a dead fox in the direction of the hunt route. Twenty-five to thirty dogs were released to follow the scent of the dead fox and then the twenty-odd riders would follow the Master of the Hunt. After the dogs, over fields owned by various landowners and farmers and separated by fences that the riders had to jump. The Master's job was also to control the rider by ordering the sounding of the trumpet to order the silence of all the riders as soon as the dogs had found the fox's lair. Then all riders would race full gallop back to the starting point.

On the hunt there were many times when the weather didn't cooperate. It wasn't pleasant being stranded in cold rainstorms without rain gear in the open fields for as long as an hour and not being able to move or make a sound without the hunt master's permission.

Any discomfort the riders suffered was soon forgotten, since after each hunt, a sumptuous lunch with refreshments awaited us on our return.

It was in 1995, ten years after purchasing Big Red that he became immobilized when the upper part of his right hind leg seemed to collapse. After treating him for twelve months, the veterinarian declared that he could no longer be ridden. Needless to say, our family was saddened by the news.

## Chapter 11
# India
# and the Elephant

On a trip to India, in 1984, I had the opportunity to try something different. While visiting the city of Jaipur, actually known as the "pink city of Jaipur," I was fortunate to discover a herd of elephants with their trainer. As soon as he spotted me as a tourist, I received an invitation to climb aboard and come for a short ride. Since he was going to sit up front and control this huge beast, and I was going to sit in the rear, I felt somewhat safe, so off we went.

I inquired as to where we were going, and he replied, "To Amber Fort," which offers fantastic views over the hills of Rajasthan. It took us forty-five minutes to reach this famous landmark, and believing my ride was over, I was ready to dismount from a height of ten or twelve feet. The trainer told me to sit still as we were now going to visit the famous palace of the wind. On our slow descent down through the residential areas, I saw first-hand why Jaipur is such a fascinating city.

Sitting on a moving elephant for two-and-a-half hours, which actually felt more like ten hours, we only covered about four kilometers. I found it quite exciting and very different from sitting on a horse's back. Getting off this huge mammal can be a harrowing experience.

I must mention that on this trip I had the opportunity to visit the city of Agra, the jumping-off point to the magnificent Taj Mahal. This extravagant memorial was built from 1630 to 1641 by Shah Jahan for his favorite wife.

India has been the land of the elephant for many centuries. I must admit, India is an exciting country. The customs, food, the many religions, beliefs, superstitions, cults that make up India's population make India a most fascinating country to visit. The three major religions are Hindu, Moslem and Sikh.

While on the back of my elephant I witnessed snake charmers and the fight between the snake's enemy, the mongoose.

The Indian elephant has been used by Indian royalty for tiger hunting and also used as a beast of burden.

Returning from Agra, I took off for Bombay and on to London for my return trip to Toronto.

A change of pace – Jaipur, India 1984

# Chapter 12

# Richochet Ranch

Richochet Ridge Ranch is located on Coast Highway 1 in the state of California, two miles north of Fort Bragg, and approximately three-and-a-half hours from the San Francisco Bay area by car. I learned of this ranch from the Equitour Company that specializes in horse vacations throughout the world. With my son Dean and his friend Shane, I flew into San Francisco and rented an auto to see the sights of San Francisco, including "The Rock" – Alcatraz. After a day-and-a-half, we headed north to visit Lari Shea, the owner of the Richochet Ranch. When we arrived at the ranch we expected to see a male owner, but instead we met a vivacious young woman, full of energy. This was the beginning of a long-lasting friendship with Lari. This was in August of 1988, a great time to visit Northern California. She matched me up with a fabulous horse named Kelly, a palomino with a smooth gait and plenty of spirit.

Lari had a different approach towards running a guest ranch. Number one, she had all her guests introduce ourselves by name, where we came from, and what experience we had in riding horses. She was the most experienced horsewoman I had ever met, not only in riding and handling horses, but also by her knowledge of veterinary care. I could tell that I could learn much from Lari.

Lari Shea has won dozens of endurance events, including the prestigious Tevis Cup 100-mile endurance race. She breeds Russian Orlov Crosses and Arabians, many of whom have excelled in dressage and jumping, as well as on competitive trails.

The quality of her horses is unbelievable.

The ride we chose was called the "redwood coast and forest trek." We would canter along deserted ocean beaches, riding the bluffs while the Pacific crashed against the rocks far below, meandering on mossy trails through the magnificent redwood forest on Northern California's rugged Mendocino Coast. This is an area of great beauty, rich in wildlife, where time flows at its own pace.

On the redwood coast ride, lodging is at the luxurious and historic Mendocino Hotel in the village and at unique bed-and-breakfast inns by the ocean, complete with elegant dining, including fine California wines, delightful hot tubs under the stars and internationally acclaimed musicians entertaining us at night.

The last day's riding fulfills a dream for many people, concluding in an hour long canter along the surf, while cormorants and osprey circle overhead and seals and whales cavort offshore. Following our dinner celebration, the farewell party culminated with entertainment by renowned Mendocino musicians. After breakfast on Sunday morning we said adios, goodbye, and started our drive back to the San Francisco Bay area.

Lari Shea also leads rides to Australia and through Kenya on a riding safari, on both of which I have joined her, as well as the Tevis 100-mile endurance seminar ride, which I will describe further on.

Ricochet Ranch, Northern California – 1988

California coast ride with "Kelly" – 1988

# Chapter 13
# Belize

My wife and I met a very interesting couple, Larry and Nancy Holtzman, when we went to Belize in Central America in January 1989, to try their so-called Jungle Ride. We made our trip through the Equitour riding trips and took off from Miami, Florida. Upon arriving in the capital city of Belize, we were met by our driver, and since we were the only people he had to meet, it wasn't long before we were in his 1985 van. The road to our campsite was like a washboard for the whole distance. My wife and I were vibrating for three hours. The driver mentioned that he has had to replace the shock absorbers at least twice a year due to the punishment his vehicle takes driving on these rough and dusty roads.

Shortly thereafter we dropped our bags off at what seemed to me quite a remote lodge, with rooms designed with thatched roofs, allowing us to see all the crawling insects, iguanas, small lizards and chameleons. We received cold refreshments to quench our thirst. We then departed for another half-hour drive along a roadway where, after a very bumpy ride, we finally approached the front gate to the ranch. The sign at the entrance read, "Mountain Equestrian Trails," and after driving along the driveway, we finally came upon our charming hosts, Larry and Nancy Holtzman.

Larry told us the story of how he came to Belize. He was a practicing dentist in Detroit, Michigan, married and doing quite well financially, when one day he picked up a copy of National Geographic and saw pictures of a country formally known as British Honduras, now known as the beautiful Belize.

He fell in love with Belize and convinced his wife to move with him. They sold his practice and left their lives behind. Six months later, she was anxious to be close to her family and realized that she was not exactly the adventurous type. Larry refused to return home, and soon after they were divorced. He met his present wife, Nancy, who actually was interested in raising cattle. They both got involved, but found it too difficult and lost their investment. Larry was not the type to give up and heard about the sale of a ranch with about six horses and a home perched high up on a hill, overlooking the entire countryside, which was all jungle.

The home was unusual, being the shape of a hexagon, giving you a view from six different angles. After his divorce, Larry and Nancy purchased the property, invested quite a bit of money and energy to build up a herd of eighteen horses, purchased used army saddles and built a small barn, then registered with Equitour as a destination for jungle horse treks. Evidently business hadn't been so great, because within minutes of meeting Larry, he handed me a real-estate broker's sales sheet offering the whole setup: home, barn, horses and some hundred acres of land all for two hundred fifty thousand dollars. He told me that he was fed up being so far from any

Jungle of Belize – 1989

86

town, with no phone or mail service. It was getting him down. His only communication with the outside world was radio communication to the lodge, where he put us up for three nights. The riding proved interesting since the guide riding directly in front of me was using a machete constantly to clear away heavy brush, bushes and overhead vines. This fast growth is due to the heavy rainfall this area gets twelve months a year. This is the reason why the trails are so muddy and tough-going. However, the beauty of Belize made up for any inconvenience I may have had.

On the ride, I was fortunate to see rare and beautiful birds, gorgeous wild orchids and huge butterflies. It is not just the natural beauty of the land that makes this ride so special, it is the abundant traces of Mayan civilization that I saw during the course of my ride. Ruins have lain covered by the jungle for more than a thousand years now, and we passed unexcavated and partially-excavated archeological sites and saw ancient pottery shards in ceremonial caves.

Lunch each day was taken beside secluded natural rock pools at the base of beautiful tropical waterfalls and, of course, there was time for swimming. Since our time of departure was quite late in the evening, we took the opportunity of visiting a small village in the neighboring country of Guatemala, famous for its Mayan ruins. I was fortunate to purchase a machete in a lovely leather case loaded with all sorts of decoration.

In case you are curious, Larry and Nancy did sell the ranch, and the new owners now call it the Mayan Jungle Ride. The last I heard was that Larry and his wife moved back to Larry's hometown, Detroit.

# Chapter 14

# *Israel*

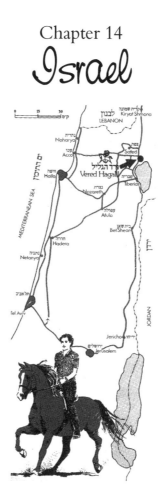

Believe it or not, a gentleman from Chicago, Illinois moved to Israel and started a horse ranch. I spent two nights there and wish to mention firstly that the name of the ranch is Vered Hagalil (The Rose of Galilee) and it's located in northern Israel, just overlooking the sea of Galilee. This is not too far from the Golan Heights, which was conquered during the 1967 war.

My first trip to Vered Hagalil was in May 1989, the perfect time to visit Israel, as the extreme heat and humidity starts in June. The guesthouse was very small and intimate, with twelve guest cottages, a two-room bunkhouse that sleeps twelve, a lounge, restaurant and swimming pool, and of course, the stables. They served a great bean soup in their restaurant, in addition to fresh fish from the lake and trout from the Dan River, and the bar is well stocked.

This was my first riding holiday in which my guide had his cell phone and a loaded pistol at his side at all times. The cell phone was used to keep in constant touch with the office in case of any emergencies and the pistol was in case of an attack from some disgruntled Arab.

Our trip down to the Sea of Galilee was slow due to the trail being very rocky and hard on the horses' hooves, but the trails led to places like the old biblical towns of Korozin and Capernaum, and to the Mount of Beatitudes where the Sermon on the Mount was given, and Tabcha, the site of the miracle of the loaves and fishes. There are not many creeks or springs in Israel, and when we came across a cool mountain spring it was all the more appreciated. We covered a lot of ground, but there is a constant unfolding of different views and since the population is sparse in this area, there was a very peaceful dimension to the day. Still, I certainly welcomed the swim in the Sea of Galilee after three or more hours in the saddle under the hot sun.

On my second day of riding, I was fortunate to be included in a documentary that was being filmed by Canadians on CBC. They had me ride my chestnut with a stripe down his nose for half-an-hour throughout the grounds, first at a walk, then a trot and closing off with a slow lope. Many of my friends and relatives recognized me when they saw it on TV. And I had the pleasure of catching it on the TV screen in 2003.

On a motor trip with my niece and nephew a few years later, we dropped in at Vered Hagalil and found a much different operation. They no longer offered riding treks away from the ranch, but instead, had a concentration of riding lessons, in Western or English saddles. I suppose the danger from possible terrorist attacks was a factor in their decision. Hopefully, by the time you read this, Israel will once again find peace and they can resume offering horse treks to the Sea of Galilee.

# Chapter 15

The first time I ever did a back-to-back trip was in 1989. The month was June and my first trip was from the thirteenth to the eighteenth, and the next was from June nineteenth to the twenty-fourth. Firstly, my chums, whom I first met in Spain, were all from the San Francisco area, and they invited me to join them on what they called the California Coast Ride. This ride was quite pleasant and the horsemen rode mostly Western-style. There are usually twenty riders and all supplies, including sleeping bags, luggage, food and various alcoholic beverages, mixes and soft drinks were carried by volunteers in their pickup trucks and trailers. The ride started in the San Mateo and Redwood City area, well known for their horse people. Instead of tennis courts, the residents usually have barns and corrals.

We headed south and passed very close to Stanford University, crossed into high mountain areas and circled back along the San Francisco Bay area. The men did all the cooking, including full breakfasts and dinners. The riders made up their own sandwiches for lunch, which were carried in the saddlebags. In the evenings, there were always some talented riders to supply guitar playing and songs and plenty of joke telling. I discovered that the campsites all had clean facilities for toilets and showers. The same for the horses. They call them horse motels, and they also have plenty of water and hoses to wash down our horses and large horse stalls for the horses to rest and eat peacefully.

The ride was for five days and since California is a long distance for me to truck my own horse, I had to rely on one of the members of this group to loan me his horse. On my first trip with these California Coast Riders, Dr. Jay Smith was kind enough to loan me his Appaloosa Esee, a well-broken gelding. Dr. Smith has since passed away. The last time I rode with him was in Mexico in 1999.

I've been invited back to ride with this group several times, and on one other occasion I witnessed a serious accident. My friend, Mr. Joe Geller, used his trailer for his own horse and the one he arranged to borrow from another group member. When we arrived at the campsite, we tied both horses to the trailer on the same side, which proved to be a serious error.

As we left the horses to pick up some hay, the two horses got into a brawl by kicking each other. One of the group members, Rick was his name, wanted to help and rushed over to the trailer to break up the fight before one of the horses could get seriously injured. Joe and I followed Rick and were about six feet behind him when he stepped between the two combatants. The horse I was going to ride gave Rick such a powerful kick that he flew into Joe, knocking him into me, and all three of us fell to the ground.

Rick got hit just below his chest on the right side, taking his breath away and leaving him with a huge red impression. We were very fortunate to have three trained paramedics along with us and I feel they saved Rick's life. Rick said that he was feeling alright and could breathe normally, and that he just wanted to rest, but looking at the bruise and checking his temperature, the paramedics felt something was wrong. They decided to call an ambulance and at the hospital they found that he was hemorrhaging internally, was losing blood, and would require an immediate operation.

After I returned to Toronto I was told that Rick would have to remain in the hospital for at least six weeks to recover, and that if he had not been brought to the hospital as soon as he was, he would not have survived. The lesson: watch out for flying hooves. Keep away from the rear of horses.

Dr. Jay Smith's Appaloosa Esee – 1989

# Chapter 16

# 100-Mile Tevis Endurance Ride

From the San Francisco airport I took off for a short flight to Sacramento, to be picked up for my next adventure, starting June nineteenth at the prestigious 100-mile Tevis Cup Endurance Ride. The Tevis Ride starts from Tahoe City, Nevada, and travels over the Sierra Nevada to Auburn, California.

The trail is steep and hazardous, with a total descent of 15,250 feet and there is a daunting 9,500-foot climb through the snowbound Squaw Pass to the El Dorado Canyon, where the temperature can reach one hundred degrees Farenheit. This endurance ride was sponsored by Lari Shea, who was already a winner of the Tevis Cup, and this trip was actually a seminar covering the whole one hundred miles in four days.

After arriving in Squaw Valley to start the ride, Lari offered me her prize Russian Orlov, Czar, a great looking gray giant of a horse. This Tevis ride is one tough ride, with the constant climbing of mountain switchbacks and then down, only to start climbing again. We spent an average of nine or ten hours each day in the saddle in late June, in sweltering heat. I didn't realize how hot it would get and how quickly I would be dehydrated. I had brought only a small canteen to hold water. It was not enough and I was constantly thirsty, and for a few days actually suffering, covering twenty-five miles at a fairly fast pace in one hundred-degree weather.

The veterinarian on full duty at all times began checking all the horses for dehydration problems, heartbeats, foot and leg soreness, etc. and when he came to Czar he found that he would not be able to continue any further. Lari quickly found me a replacement, a four-year-old green horse, who also became sick and extremely tired four or five hours before the finish line. I removed his saddle after dismounting and had to walk with my English boots on. A very understanding gentleman who had sneakers on offered me his horse, and since back home he walked five miles each morning, he didn't mind walking to the conclusion of the ride.

Each night we slept in different campsites, with riders bringing tents or sleeping bags. At the end of each day's ride we had to cool off our mounts, and if they refused to drink water, electrolytes were force-fed into their mouths to make up their salt loss and perhaps make them thirsty enough to drink water.

We riders cooled off by drinking our choice of ice-cold refreshments, including soft drinks, water, beer, choice of fruit and Gatorade drinks. Cocktails were also available, providing we made our own. On one evening, all the riders were shown a video of the Tevis being done on foot – that's right, no horses, and that's done one week before the mounted riders start. I recall that some of the trails were so steep for the horses to climb that the riders had to dismount, get behind their horses, and hang on to their tails to help themselves climb up.

All horses were taken to comfortable quarters at the completion. Each and every horse received a cool shower, which I'm sure they appreciated, and a few apples and carrots. All the riders that completed the Tevis attended a farewell dinner, and each of us received a certificate stating we had completed the Tevis, dated and signed by Lari Shea. I feel very proud to have received this certificate, as this was, I felt, a great accomplishment. There aren't too many Canadian riders that I've heard of that have ever entered this particular 100-mile endurance ride. Today, stringent checks by veterinarians take place at intervals throughout the course, and entry is limited to qualified riders.

California Endurance Ride

# Chapter 17
# The Equitour Experience

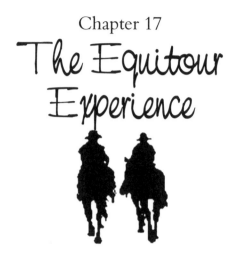

The man in charge of the Equitour World Wide Riding Holidays catalogue is Mr. Bayard Fox. Equitours offers various types of riding holidays in countries such as New Zealand, India, Turkey, Chile, France, Iceland and Morocco.

I met Bayard for the first time in 1990, when I visited his ranch in Wyoming, called Bitterroot. His wife, Mel, runs the Bitterroot Ranch very professionally. All the guests are lodged in good-sized cabins, all equipped with showers and toilets and cleaned every day. Students from nearby schools staff the kitchen and dining room, and all the wranglers who handle the horses work in the barn. The riding is well organized, giving riders a choice of three different rides: slow, fast and for experienced riders only. Each day the rides begin at 10:00 A.M. until 12:00 noon and again at 2 P.M. until 4:30 P.M. The dinner bell rings at 6:00 P.M. for wine and cheese and a nice selection of hors d'oeuvres, and dinner promptly begins at seven.

I had a conversation with Bayard in the dining room and I inquired about all the destinations he serves and who scouts these places for him. He said that since he was over sixty-five, he had decided to leave the checking-out to one or two members of his staff. I suggested to Bayard that since I was only sixty-one and retired, I could offer my services. My willingness to travel

Bitterroot Ranch

anywhere to research potential clients and scout new places for the brochure made him consider my proposal.

Shortly after the meeting, Bayard called and told me about a couple who ran a riding school and lodge and wanted to be included in Equitour's future brochures. I inquired about the location, and he replied that it was in Peterborough. I was quite pleased since Peterborough is only eighty-five miles east of Toronto; however, when I called to ask for directions, I thought I had the wrong number. He told me to head in the direction of Vermont, and then I realized I was heading to Peterborough located in the state of New Hampshire.

I then called my local CAA club to get road maps, and off I went into a new adventure and a career as an investigator of horse handlers. After a ten-hour auto journey, I finally arrived at Honey Lane Farms, located in Dublin, New Hampshire. I must say, I was very impressed with their accommodation and would judge it as a four-star establishment. My hosts were Mr. and Mrs. Coutu, a very warm couple who go above and beyond for their guests' happiness. They have a fine barn with an indoor arena right next door. Their mounts are first-class, well-bred horses, and their equipment well maintained. I thoroughly enjoyed the trail riding in heavily wooded areas, and I felt as if I were a hundred miles from anywhere. I gave the Honey Lane Farms high marks for anyone looking for a quiet horse vacation.

My next trip for Equitour was in Puerto Vallarta at the Rancho Ojo De Aqua run by a very wealthy Mexican dentist, who had a "horse for hire by the hour" operation. He wanted to expand his business by offering horse treks for one week up the Sierra Madre Mountains.

Dr. Octavio Gonzales, who spoke excellent English, met me at the airport. After arriving at his home, I was introduced to his wife and young son, Alberto. I was taken on a tour of his premises and ended up on a one-hour trail ride with a small group. It was the end of April, which is a great time to visit Mexico as it is not too hot at that time. After a delicious dinner made by his wife, the doctor told me that he had no space in his home for at least two days and asked if I would mind staying in a downtown hotel. The two days that I spent downtown gave me the opportunity to do some sightseeing and indulge in Mexican cuisine. Dr. Gonzalez picked me up in the morning at the Sheraton Hotel and brought me back to his home, where his wife, Mari, prepared a fabulous

Sierra Madre Mountain – Puerto Vallarte

lunch. After lunch we discussed his plans for our journey to his campsite high up in the Sierra Madre Mountains where he planned to take his guests on horseback.

The first fact that any visitor learns about Puerto Vallarta is that the tiny fishing village was put on the map by the merry-making of Richard Burton and Elizabeth Taylor. Ever since Burton filmed *The Night of the Iguana* in 1963, the story has figured in all of the guidebooks. In the passing years, with the explosion of mass tourism, the gulf between the two Mexico's has only grown. Nowadays, there are few places where the real Mexico has been so pushed aside as in Puerto Vallarta, with its strip malls, gated condo communities and franchise operations – Hooters is the latest arrival, just across from the lone cathedral.

Puerto Vallarta has more in common with south Florida than with its neighbors down the *carretera*. In the past ten years tourism has increased by about 50% to almost 3 million visitors per year, and I was surprised to find at least a half dozen horse ranches offering horseback rides by the hour, half-day and full day.

After a good night's sleep in his home, Dr. Gonzales and I started our trip early. With our lunches and drinks packed in our saddlebags, this was to be an all-day ride, climbing the Sierra Madre Mountains (once captured by the brutal conquistadors). At first the climb was gradual, but after a few hours the trail began to get very steep and I was beginning to tire from leaning forward in the saddle and keeping my butt off the horse's back. We eventually stopped for lunch and also to give the horses a well-deserved rest.

Climbing steep hills for a long time can be very tiring for a horse, even though he does have four legs. Dr. Gonzales told me that after another hour of tough climbing, we were going to change our mounts and travel on donkeys, since the trail begins to get very perilous, and they are the most sure-footed animals on treks. The donkey that he obtained for me was so short my legs were almost touching the ground. Eventually, we arrived at the top of the mountain. I will do my best to describe what I found there. On a flat area he had ten tents set up, and each one was furnished with a double mattress. Nearby was a new building that housed flush toilets for both men and women, shower stalls and sinks with running hot and cold water. At the entrance of this private small village was an open-air stone barbeque, with a dozen tables and chairs that made up the dining quarters, and not far away was a large round aboveground cement swimming pool. There was no barn or building or shed to hold the horses or donkeys, except for two 16 ft. poles tied down on wooden posts to act as a tie-down with no overhead shelter. I wasn't overly impressed with this destination for guests spending anywhere from $800 to $1,200 for this ride. After a good night's sleep and breakfast the next morning, we started our journey back down the mountain, first with the donkey and then back on my mount. It took us eight hours to return to the doctor's residence, and I suppose the doctor felt that I wasn't too keen on his trek, as his personality suddenly changed towards me. Believe it or not, I never saw him again after we removed the saddles from the backs of the horses. As I entered his home, his wife Mari told me that there was no dinner prepared, and would I mind eating at a local restaurant, which I did. When I returned to their home, Mari informed me that the doctor could not drive me to the airport the following morning and that I should arrange for a taxi. That night I worked on my report for the Equitour brochure and I gave this ride a thumb's down. Bayard Fox accepted my decision.

I must mention that in the doctor's home I saw a beautiful hand-crafted Mexican wooden saddle, and enquired if it was possible to order the same exact saddle and have it shipped to Canada. Mari said that if I left her the payment in full, she would make the arrangements to have the saddle sent to me. I did just that, and after five months of phoning and waiting, the saddle finally arrived, and I now use it in my home as a decorative piece of furniture.

# Chapter 18

# Portugal

**M**y next investigative trip took place in July, and the destination was to be Italy. By sheer coincidence, I had already booked a trip through Equitour for my daughter Nadine and I to travel to Portugal, and I could not have planned things any better. I would go riding in Portugal, see my daughter off at the airport for her return to Toronto, and continue on to Italy. Since this was all going to take place during the month of July, I could not imagine what I was getting myself into as far as the heat was concerned. Nadine and I took off for Lisbon, and upon our arrival, we checked into the Ritz Carlton Hotel as arranged by Bayard Fox. We spent a full day sight-seeing. Our pick-up was the following morning, and off we went to see the horses in the small village of Alcaina where the Escola de Equitacao is located. The selection of horses was made, for a change in an indoor arena, and the horse chosen for me was called *Cite*. Our guide was a young, strong, well-built fellow by the name of Manuel. This ride was for one week and took place just north west of Lisbon in an area called Estoril, and the two main villages that we entered were Mafra and Sintra. The riding group consisted of ten people made up of Americans, two Canadians and Europeans. The only problem that I had was the heat and more heat, to the point of being unbearable at times. I recall one night fighting off mosquitoes while trying to sleep, and another so hot and humid, I moved my bed so that I could put my head out the window, and even that did not help. Finally, as a last resort, I took cold showers almost every hour. The most exciting experience that Nadine and I witnessed was the bull

"End of World Ride" – Portugal
Milfontes – starting point

Portugal with Nadine (Atlantic Ocean) – Portugal

fighting in Portugal, where the bull is not killed, or should I say, butchered. Actually, in the Lisbon bullring there were plenty of laughs, unlike the bullring in Madrid. When the bull is released, he is met by toreadors who are lined up one behind the other single-file, and when the bull attacks, naturally the one in front takes the full brunt of the attack, and this continues on for at least another few bull attacks, with the front man getting pretty banged up. The seven men finally break up and start to tease the animal, grabbing him by his tail and horns and finally wrestling him to the ground. That front man must either be very brave or crazy! Other than the excessive heat, the ride in Portugal, according to my daughter, was a lot of fun, and we did meet some very nice people. Well, it was now time to move on. Nadine and I shared a taxi to the Lisbon airport as our flights were leaving at almost the same time.

# Chapter 19
## *Italy*

After seeing my daughter off, I went to catch my flight to Rome and found everything at the check-in counter in chaos. The luggage belt had broken down, and all the luggage was piling up behind the check-in clerk. At that moment I felt that my baggage would not arrive in Italy, when I did. My flight on Alitalia Airlines was short, and sure enough, my luggage was missing when I arrived, which presented quite a problem for me as all my riding gear, including my riding boots, was now missing. I filled out all the proper forms and put down Grosseto as my destination since this was the last train stop. My actual destination was a small medieval village called Scansano. My host-to-be was a chap by the name of Massimo, who had a hotel a few miles from Scansano and decided to get into the horse business. With plenty of space to spare at his hotel, which he called Antica Casale, he decided to build an up-to-date stable filled with good riding horses and an extra large riding ring (corral). Massimo's plan was grandiose. Since he had the hotel with an excellent chef, located in the beautiful Tuscany area, he wanted to conduct horse treks throughout his region for guests that would stay at the hotel, enjoy the well-prepared food and ride to their heart's content. He contacted the Equitour office, and in turn, Bayard contacted me to check out the facilities at Antica Casale.

At my arrival in Rome, I transferred by bus to the main train station, which I found in utter confusion as I attempted to buy a ticket to Grossetto, which was not easy. Remember, this was still July, and still hot, and even hotter on the train where the cars had no air-conditioning. I arrived very late in the evening, and after one hour of trying to call Massimo by phone. I finally reached him and told him that I had arrived and if he could arrange for someone to pick me up. Massimo himself picked me up. He spoke English very well and gave me a short tour of Grossetto. I was surprised at the size of this small city, which was very lively, with many cafes lining the brightly lit streets even though it was close to midnight. After a forty-five-minute drive on winding, unlit roads, we arrived at the Antica Casale Hotel, which I learned had once been an old barn. My host had it converted into a hotel at great expense. It was quite charming, with a large outdoor patio where dinner was served, overlooking a mountainside covered with olive trees. The patio could be protected from the rain with a large, electrically operated awning.

The next morning, Massimo and I met for breakfast on the outdoor patio, and we discussed strategy for the rides. I told him that American guests would prefer a seven-day trip with six days of riding. The accommodations were excellent and it seemed that with his handpicked chef the guests would be in their glory for the evening candlelit dinners. So far, so good. I also explained that he would need a different destination and trail every day so that the guests would have something to look forward to.

After breakfast we took a short downhill walk to the stable area where he had ten well-groomed horses in clean, large, bright stalls. The tack room where the saddles were stored was clean and organized to the point that each saddle had etched into it the name of the horse it belonged to. This to me seemed like a five-star operation.

Now the trails! Massimo fulfilled his promise; every day we traveled different routes, eating lunch in small, quaint village bars or restaurants, visiting Roman ruins, vineyards, olive plantations

Scansano, Italy

and the hot thermal springs at Saturnia. And best of all was the medieval village of Scansano, where he would take me in the evenings to the outdoor restaurant with overhead lines of colored light bulbs, where they served Amaro Montenegro, a sweet-tasting aperitif with a dish of Italian ice cream. During my stay with Massimo at his hotel, we would meet each afternoon for vodka on the rocks and discuss the business end of this new venture he was trying to break into. We talked about the minimum and maximum number of riders he would accept, the fee he would charge and the responsibility of picking up the guests from the Rome airport and then returning them a week later. Also, in the event that a rider received injuries from a fall, where were the nearest medical facilities?

During my stay, Massimo invited me to his home for a brunch and the opportunity to meet his wife and two daughters. I was surprised when he took me to the rear of his home to show me where he had built a winery, including a large modern building with a half-dozen stainless-steel vats and a full-scale bottling line. This man was certainly ambitious. Each day at the hotel I would find an hour to write of what I saw and did and send it off to Equitour when I returned to Canada. In my report I highly recommended the Antica Casale for a riding vacation. I am very sad to report that I heard that Massimo had lost his financial interest in the hotel, and possibly his wine operation also, just eighteen months after I had visited. I mentioned earlier that my luggage had not arrived at the Rome airport. Well, it finally did show up at the train station in Grosseto.

# Chapter 20
# Africa

I could feel the excitement in the air as we were heading for the vast plains of the beloved country of Hemingway and Blixen, the land of the fiercely proud Masai and the home of zebras, lions, giraffes, gazelles and mighty elephants. We were told that our itinerary would include riding over the lovely "Loita Hills" into the Masai Mara game reserve, over rivers, across the Mara Plains and through the acacia-forested Lemek Valley.

The drive to meet our horses took an hour-and-a-half. My horse's name was King Kong. The ride began through dense bushes with thorns three inches long. That first day out we saw wildebeest, vervet monkeys, impala and wild parrots. The horses seemed quite accustomed to the game animals and even enjoyed chasing them at times.

On our second and third day we came across zebra, which our horses enjoyed chasing. There were also plenty of giraffe. Each and every evening tents were set up with comfortable cots placed inside. The third day brought plenty of excitement when we were passing through tall grassy lion country (and our guides did not carry pistols or rifles). Suddenly, three spare horses from the rear came galloping to the front of the column, spooking and

Taking blood for a drink

scaring all the riders' horses. They in turn all bolted full speed forward. Looking to the rear I saw a huge lioness dart between the trees.

I will never forget that sight. All the horses were bolting and racing forward at great speed when suddenly, Paddy screamed at the top of his lungs, "Stop and slow down, otherwise the lioness could attack." Evidently we must have crossed the path of her cubs. We were told to go slowly forward, which we did, while holding a tight rein, as the horses were very excited. I still can't believe it.

All of the riders said the same thing – their hearts dropped at the sight of the huge lioness. We also saw a pack of wild dogs, which is a very rare sight as they are becoming extinct.

This Kenya endurance horse safari was the most thrilling and exciting trip I have ever been on. Lari Shea from the Ricochet organized this trip, which started in March of 1990. I kept a diary; my fellow participants were Lari Shea and John from California, Mike from Philadelphia, Ruth from Las Vegas, Harvey and his young son, Eric, and our great guide Paddy and his assistant Raymond. All of us had to take malaria pills two weeks before the ride started, again during the two-week safari and a further two weeks after we left Africa.

The trip began when we all met at the charming Norfolk Hotel, with its huge outdoor veranda in the front where guests gathered for drinks and light snacks. I remember the unusual name of the street the hotel was located on – Harry Thuku Road – and further down the street was the Boulevard Hotel. After I and the other riders had arrived, we were told that since there had been heavy rainfalls for the past few days, the road getting to our campsite was a total washout, and therefore, we

Visiting Masai Tribe Village – Kenya, Africa

Group photo – Kenya, Africa

had to remain in Nairobi for at least two days. I didn't mind as it gave me the opportunity for some sightseeing in the capital city of Kenya. The Republic of Kenya is situated on the east coast of Africa and occupies a total land area of 580,367 square kilometers.

The first observation I made while walking through the downtown area of Nairobi is that Indians from India owned at least ninety percent of the stores. I also found it quite safe walking during the daylight hours, but was warned to take taxis in the evening. After two days of taking in the sights, I found Nairobi quite a cosmopolitan city, with many religions represented, including Judaism, Seventh Day Adventist, Catholicism, Islam and Greek Orthodoxy. There are at least fifty hotels, large commercial high-rise buildings, cinemas and theatres, cultural centers and libraries. On March 16 we finally got the call to pack up and be ready to leave for the ride of a lifetime in the Ambroseli National Park, home of the Masai people and an area of hot, dry, thornbush country where big game animals can be observed against a backdrop of the snow-capped peaks of Mount Kilimanjaro.

On the fourth and fifth days we stopped at two Masai villages where they offered their wares of beads, bracelets, necklaces and arrow containers. They enjoy the bargaining and can use the American dollars to purchase materials for their clothing. Their huts are constructed out of cow dung.

On the following three or four days our group saw baboons, water buffalo and a spitting cobra, which can spit into your eyes while you are on horseback and blind you for a few hours.

Our next campsite was on the banks of the Mara River where plenty of hippos were enjoying a swim. During the next few days we came across a herd of approximately fifty elephants, including their young, as well as bull elephants, which are very dangerous when disturbed. Walking through the dense brush, knocking down trees, we approached cautiously, inching in a little at a time. One bull elephant kept eyeing us. John got a little too close and the bull elephant trumpeted and came after us. Our horses got excited again and we galloped away. All I could hear was those big feet pounding the earth behind me. Again Paddy told us to slow down as the horses could have tripped over the branches of trees

Chasing giraffe – Kenya Horse Safari

Lari Shea and Friends

lying on the ground, throwing the riders off and getting trampled by the elephants.

At 8:00 A.M. we said goodbye to our staff. The staff consisted of eight black employees who set up our camps, including the showers and toilets. They also set up our dining quarters for breakfast and dinners, cooked meals, did the laundry and loaded and unloaded our luggage when necessary. We had a rougher day getting out of the Mara than any day on horseback.

We got out just in time, as the rain had started again. After two-and-a-half hours of muddy roads, we got to Narok for gas. We ate lunch on the side of the road in the Rift Valley, then crossed the equator and went to Naruru (entrance to the Flamingo Park). We got there about 4:30 P.M. and when we left for Lake Baringo it was dark and raining. We crossed the lake in a small, flat-bottomed boat passing hippos and alligators all around us. We landed in the dark at a quaint village where we had a great buffet with flute music and Masai dancers.

Just a few more words about the Masai: to the Masai people, cattle are the most cherished thing in their lives, next to a child or a plot of land. A cow is far more to them than a source of meat or milk. The Masai, who wear bright red tunics and elaborate multi-colored jewelry, stand out among Kenya's more than forty tribes for the high leaps of their traditional dances. In ceremonies, they drink the blood of the cow, mixing it with honey beer, and they use every inch of the animal for clothing and decorations. Each man pays the father of the girl he wants to marry in cows, and even the dung of the cow is put to use as lacquer to protect the outside of their huts. The cow is almost the center of their lives, it's sacred, and it's more than property. They give them names, and even talk to them, and they perform rituals with them. The Masai have a reputation as warriors, developed in the colonial days when they fought those who trod on their rangeland. The tribe still teaches the young men to fight and they are circumcised at the age of fourteen without any anesthetic. It is now illegal for the Masai to hunt lions, which had been a rite of passage for young men. Nowadays, television sets are appearing in their huts.

## Chapter 21
# The Down Under Trip

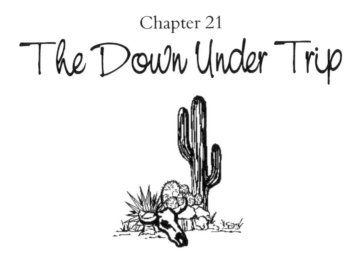

I t was Lari Shea who convinced me to take the Australia horse ride when she mentioned that a portion of the ride would take place in the Snowy River Country. I had seen the movie "The Man From Snowy River," and I could relate to the adventure to be had. Our group traveling direct from Los Angeles to Sydney consisted of twenty Americans and me, the lone Canadian. As luck would have it, I arrived without luggage. The $60 cash voucher from Quantas Airlines provided me with a few shirts, underwear, socks and a toothbrush. The facilities in San Michelle were quite pleasant. Our host and guide, Mr. Snow Minor, owned a small motel with a fully equipped kitchen and a well-stocked bar.

Two days later, my luggage was found and shipped to me in Sydney right before we flew off to Cooma, where we would later take a bus to San Michelle. This portion of the ride was only for four days as it was fly-biting season, and they were constantly swarming around the horses and riders, making both parties unbearable company. Furthermore, the pace was slow, very slow at times, due to the two-pack horse that accompanied us carrying all the supplies.

I was pleased to ride with three familiar figures, Ruth, Lari Shea and Harvey (carrying over a romance started in Kenya!).

Included in this large group was a fellow from New Jersey, Dan Capone, who had a great knack for telling jokes. Dan and I hit it off immediately. We have become friends and, in fact, he later joined me on a cattle drive at the TX in Montana. Dan and his wife, Rosalie, also motored to Toronto for a visit and attended the famous yearly Royal Winter Fair horse show, featuring world-class international horse jumping events. We also met on a horse trek in Turkey that I organized in June 2000.

The horse chosen for me on this snowy river country ride was a full-blooded Australian-bred gelding named Hero. Appropriately named, he contended with the unrelenting heat, hard dry trails and millions of horrible flies, which he desperately tried to shake off.

We rode to the area of the Yarrango Billy Caves and actually had the opportunity to dismount and visit the caves and the thermal pool. I was lost in the richness of this captivating sight and felt fortunate and thankful to be there; however, on the fourth day, an unexpected bout of dehydration set in. We all took advantage of a quick flowing stream, and our guide suggested we drink from it – something we would later learn to regret.

We were lucky, as that same evening we flew out of Cooma to Brisbane and checked into a four-star hotel. Dan Capone and I shared a double room but neither of us got to use the beds, as we took turns the whole night suffering with diarrhea. Dan was very concerned that we would become dehydrated, and in the early morning we discovered that the whole group had come down with dysentery, cramps and headaches. We all agreed to have a doctor come to the hotel immediately. The doctor said that the same bug from the water we drank attacked us all. Pills were distributed to all of us and we used the two-day visit in Brisbane to regain our strength for the next adventure, the infamous rainforest, noted for all sorts of insects, spiders and snakes.

We spent six days in the Conondale Rainforest in the Conondale Range, on a ride called the Queensland Trek, run by a fantastic horseman, Mr. Bob Sample. This ride was unique because all the horses were trained to the hackamore bridle, meaning that none of the horses required a bridle or a bit in their mouths to control movements. Never before, or after this ride, have I came across a ranch or riding stable that caters to guests who ride horses without a bridle or a bit.

We certainly received our share of rain, but were thankfully protected by the thick forest of tall trees covered with leaves. Every night we pitched our small two-man tents accordingly. Again, my sleeping partner was Dan Capone, but his snoring was so unbearably loud that it was impossible to fall asleep. I decided to pull my bag out into the open field at least fifty feet away from snoring Dan. Because it was very dark, I didn't realize that I was under a tree with low branches, and when I awoke I found myself staring at a huge black spider hanging from his web staring right at me. I didn't move. I couldn't move. I was praying that I wouldn't be bitten by a possibly poisonous spider. Dan heard my cries, picked up a long stick and removed the spider from my face.

Each morning we had the company of the noisiest bird in the world, the kookaburra. This bird is small, but with an unusually

Saucy & Loud – Kookaburra

Visit by a Python Snake

deafening sound that would even drown out the noisy, snoring Dan.

My mount was Houdini and I was very pleased that he was steady and didn't spook too easily. On the fourth day out on the trail I couldn't believe my eyes when I spotted, just a few feet in front of me, a gigantic snake slithering along. I called out to Bob and he came quickly, picked up the snake and brought him over to me. He explained that this snake was a python approximately fifteen feet long and would not bite, but rather, would wrap himself around me and squeeze me to death!

Finally, the last day of our trek we left the rain forest and arrived at an open green range area. This was where I saw many jumping kangaroos for the first time. These kangaroos were truly a sight to behold, with their large hindquarters and short front legs, moving quickly with every jump.

The third portion of our trip down under was a very pleasant surprise. It was a short flight on a five-passenger propeller plane to Musket Cove on Malolo Laila Island in the Fiji Islands, where we rested for two days. We had great accommodations in large thatched-roofed cottages with two-bedroom suites, kitchen and bar. We also had the choice of swimming in the Pacific or the large saltwater swimming pool. The resort was well maintained, with a four-star restaurant justly proud of its stock of choice Australian shiraz wines. The weather was just divine and the riders had a choice of returning to Sydney or carrying on for another five days on a chartered cruise. Dan and I chose to fly to Nadia, a busy and thriving Fijian town where we enjoyed a lunch of various delicious Chinese dishes. Our next flight was to Sydney, Australia and then to the Hawaiian Islands, finally arriving on the west coast of Canada. After eighteen hours in total, we arrived in Toronto.

# Chapter 22
# A Change for a Change

Instead of riding horses, I decided back in 1987 to race them for a change. Bernie Ottaway was a friend of mine from way back in 1958. He had a riding academy on the outskirts of Toronto. Like everyone else, with the expansion of the city, he moved to the countryside just south of my present farm. He continued boarding horses as well as training and raising three sons, one of whom, Brian, became a professional thoroughbred horse trainer.

I phoned Brian and told him of my wishes to get involved with racing horses and asked him if he could offer any suggestions. He told me he could and explained that the best and cheapest way for a beginner to get involved was to claim a horse, which would put me into the business immediately. I agreed and asked him to explain what claiming a horse meant, and how to work it. Every day, I found out, there are always two, three or four claiming races that can start at eight thousand dollars and go up to forty thousand dollars, depending on the horse's condition and past track record, and perhaps his breeding. These races are for owners who want to dispose of their horses for various reasons. The horses must be claimed before the race starts. In other words, if you claim a horse and he breaks his leg during the race, you are out of luck.

I told him he could claim a horse for me with a limit of ten thousand dollars since many other expenses will be accrued later, such as training fees, stabling and feeding, purchasing colors for a jockey, etc. Before I knew it, Brian called me and said he'd claimed a five-year-old horse named Joust Up for eighty-five

Joust Up

hundred dollars. He was sound but did not have the best track record, needed to put on some weight and would require a lot of work. Little did I know that in just a few short weeks, Joust Up, with his new colors of light and dark blue, which I took from a cigarette package, would come in third. On his second try for me he put me in the winner's circle and what a thrill that was! On his next race, the trainer put him in a claiming race, which he won and, of course, I lost him as some other party claimed him from me. All told I came out with a net profit of fifteen thousand dollars – not bad for a beginner.

I thought to myself, if I purchased a more expensive horse, I could enter him in a higher stakes race and make a fortune, perhaps sixty or every one hundred thousand dollars. You see… that's where greed comes in. Since I was an inexperienced winner, I decided to go big time by going to the yearling auction sale without my trainer. That was my first among many errors. Never try to purchase a thoroughbred horse on your own. Always take an experienced trainer and/or veterinarian.

When I arrived at the yearling sale (the horses are only twelve months old), I received a complete list of the colts and fillies that were to be auctioned off that evening. This list gives a total history of each horse, his background, the stud and mare: in other words, his bloodline, which might go back one, two or three generations.

Checking out the blood lines, I discovered a colt that had some of Northern Dancer's blood and decided to bid up to ten thousand dollars. His sire was well-decorated, and the dam was Kennissis. The bidding began at five thousand dollars and interest fell off around nine thousand dollars. I thought I had a bargain at fourteen thousand dollars.

I phoned my trainer, Brian, who arranged for the pick-up of my new opportunity to make a million. I named the horse *Smote Them*, paid twelve hundred dollars a month for eighteen months, plus vet checks, specially fitted shoes, supplement feeds, etc. The end result was that Smote Them never even made it to the track to race. The reason was that both his front legs gave out.

I sold this horse for $100, which made for a total loss of thirty-five thousand dollars, but I was fortunate that this time I had two partners with whom to share the loss.

I wasn't about to give up, however. I completely went against my wife's advice that I should not get seriously into this sport, just have fun and keep my investments as low as possible, trust luck – after all, that's what racing is all about, luck. I thought that if I purchased another yearling at a higher price, I would have a much better chance of acquiring a winner. That was another mistake.

I purchased my colt in September, 1998 on appearance only. He was a tall, good-looking chestnut, three white stockings and blaze down his nose, and this time I upped the ante to eighteen thousand dollars, without any partners. Again, the monthly training expenses with easy workouts so we wouldn't take a chance hurting his legs, and the best of feed. The horse came out of good breeding stock, the sire being Assert and the dam Shanghai Melody. I named him after my first-born grandson, Samalorn.

Samalorn at a cost of $18,000

I was very excited as we were fast approaching the racing season and I was looking forward to banking perhaps two million dollars. The horrible truth was that he also didn't make it to the track because of leg problems and I sold him to a friend for one thousand dollars. This last transaction cost me a cool forty thousand dollars and a taught me a good lesson. I have never gone back to the track or gotten involved with race horses again. I'll stick to riding horses, not racing them. I learned, later on, that only one horse out of a hundred will make it to the track from the yearling stage.

# Chapter 23
# Unusual Destination

I t was in St. Moritz on a ski vacation with my wife that I found a great riding stable where they supplied the horses for the famous "Race on Ice." This is where the jockey doesn't ride on the back of the horse, but instead, wearing a pair of skis on his feet and goggles on his eyes, he goes behind the horse and grabs on to just a set of thirty-foot reins. The jockeys attempt to stay upright while being pulled at thirty to forty miles per hour around an oval track of frozen lake. These races are run weekly during the month of February, and if you are as fortunate as we were, you can see them race from the rear balcony of any hotel situated close to the frozen lake. The stable also provided horses for riding enthusiasts, as well as guides. I thoroughly enjoyed my ski vacation that week in 1987, as I would split the two sports each day by skiing in the morning and horseback riding after lunch in the beautiful forests surrounding St. Moritz.

Who could believe that, on a ski trip to the Italian ski slopes of Cortina, I could also include horse riding in my agenda? My wife, Zuzik, and I, along with another couple, Mr. and Mrs. Gaston Botero, decided to take a winter holiday in 1990 in Cortina, Italy, where the peaks of the Dolomite Mountains can rise to fifteen thousand feet. At the front desk of our hotel, I inquired whether there were any riding academies nearby. To my surprise, the answer was yes. I immediately arranged for my pick-up, and I arrived at the stable in approximately thirty minutes. To my amazement, I found a thirty-horse stable. It was clean and well managed, it seemed, by professionals. The horse they chose for me was actually pure white and seemed quite comfortable in the high altitudes. What else but a romantic name could have been chosen for this frisky fellow, whose name was Romeo. Romeo and I rode around the nearby forests on snow-covered ground that day and when we got back I made arrangements for transportation to and from the stable every afternoon for the next six days. As far as I was concerned, this turned out to be a super winter vacation.

St. Moritz Singea

126

# Chapter 24
# Unusual Destinations: Jordan

T he most unusual ride that I ever experienced was in the country of Jordan – my camel ride. The rose-red city of Petra is one of the most fascinating places on earth. After a three-hour drive from Amman in a straight southerly direction, we reached our destination, but not before driving down a long, winding, dusty road in the summer heat of June. The driver of our minibus stopped abruptly and told us we would have to continue by foot, or hire a horse or camel from a choice of many Bedouin guides, to navigate the 1.2 kilometers through the mountain gorge, known as the Siq. I chose a camel.

Paying less than twenty Canadian dollars, we embarked on a road that was first built by the Nabateans and later reconstructed by the Romans. Temperatures reached well over thirty degrees Celsius, so walking through hot sand in an area below sea level required us to be prepared. My thoughts turned to the British officer, Lawrence of Arabia, who said that water is the most precious commodity in this part of the world.

It seemed as though the path was eternal until we were greeted by a glimpse of Petra, beckoning with ornate pillars, soaring portico and a central urn, all carved out of a mountain of swirling rose sandstone.

Petra

On camel back for a change

This is the Khazneh, or treasury, the most intricately chiseled façade in the city of mountains, temples and tombs. These structures date back as far as two thousand three hundred years, each one carved by hand. This was the remarkably preserved showpiece of an empire dating to 6 B.C.E. It would eventually fall to the Romans around 100 C.E., which explains the remains of an eight thousand-seat amphitheatre and a Roman colonnade. The last climactic scenes of *Indiana Jones and the Final Crusade* were shot there.

The city of Petra is quite large and it is important to wear comfortable shoes or boots as there is much to explore and heights to climb. The largest is the Monastery, only a few steps away from a panoramic vista that to the west overlooks the Dead Sea and beyond which lies the hills of Judea and Jerusalem.

On leaving Petra I was fairly tired and decided to return to our awaiting minivan by camel again, instead of choosing a horse. When we arrived at the hotel, I decided to leave my wife for a short time and have a short horseback ride into the Siq, just for the experience.

# Chapter 25

# Florida

Back in 1990, while vacationing in North Miami Beach, when most vacationers were sunbathing, boating and golfing, I checked to see whether there were any riding facilities in the area. Much to my amazement, I discovered a town called Davie, the heart of the horse community.

I was quite disappointed to find that most riding academies were closed for business; however, on one expedition I noticed two large cement statues of horses on either side of a driveway. Little did I know, but I had stumbled upon the Spun Gold Equestrian Centre, a place that would end up being a safe haven for me and my home away from home. Along a driveway lined on both sides with white board fences stood a jumping ring, a pretty bungalow home with a barn and an outdoor training circle. There was more acreage in the rear of the property, and it seemed to be a well-planned operation.

I stopped in the driveway of the bungalow and was met by the owner, Lynn. She gave riding lessons, drove her own large horse trailers to distant horse shows for her many clients, ordered feed, hay, and grain, and looked after her many pets, including dogs and cats. In addition, she was raising a young daughter and supervised a place where I could ride. She immediately wanted to know what experience I had in riding and said she did not rent horses out by the hour; however, she did have a few boarders who liked to see their horses exercised every day. She then told me the best news of all. Very close to her stables is the fifteen hundred acre Tree Tops Park, which has miles of horse trails that I could explore, plus horse showers, clean washrooms, toilets and telephones.

We worked out a schedule for two rides each week and, to save time, she would deliver the horse I would ride right to the park, leave me there for three or four hours, and then pick up the horse, provided I would supply my own saddle and bridle and pay her the going rate. The schedule is still ongoing, and whether I visit Florida for a month or four months, Lynn is there looking after my equestrian needs. She is certainly one hell of a great gal. Over the years I have managed to ride many of her clients' horses in the Tree Tops Park, enjoying picking oranges off the trees while riding, trotting through lovely sandy trails and taking the odd gallop in jungle-like forests. Thank heaven for a person like Lynn. I must mention that she has already given my six-year-old grandson lessons in riding for the past two years.

Spun Gold Equestrian Centre

## Chapter 26

# Unusual Destinations: New Mexico

Taking a trip to the state of New Mexico is not unusual, however, after reading the advertisement in 1997 from a guest ranch that has over one thousand head of cattle roaming around that required gathering, my son Mory and I decided to pay the N. Bar Ranch a visit. After landing in Albuquerque and then taking a pleasant drive to Santa Fe, visiting the many antique and art shops, we decided to stay overnight in Santa Fe. In the morning after breakfast we drove straight south towards the N. Bar Ranch, which is actually close to the Mexican Border.

My son and I had a pleasant surprise when we saw the accommodations: well-constructed log cabins, with single or twin beds. Since there weren't too many guests,

N. Bar Ranch – 1997

we each had our own cabin, nicely furnished with floor carpets, stove and a dresser. There were showers close by, and food was served in a large kitchen/dining room combined. What made this trip unusual was that the owner/guide and the few guests spent the whole week looking for this herd of one thousand cows, and finally, on the fourth day found seven cows. The owner claimed that his ranch covered such a vast area that perhaps that was the reason we could not find his herd of cattle. To make up for not seeing his big bunch of cows he would personally take us by horseback on a tour of his ranch.

I must admit that I had never pictured New Mexico to be so beautiful. I thought I would see a lot of desert and sand. Instead I saw forests, rolling hills, huge areas of growing waving wheat – just a great landscape. Each evening our host supplied entertainment with guest country singers and guitarists.

Mory and Hy – New Mexico

# Chapter 27

# End of the World Ride: Portugal

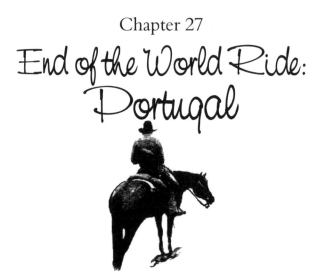

I n early October of 1996, I received a call from my friend Joe Geller of San Francisco that his buddies would like me to join them on a ride in the southern part of Portugal. I accepted immediately since the southwest of Portugal is ideally suited to trail riding, and the climate in October is exceptionally temperate. This area is one of the least populated parts of Europe and has been protected by law from the unbridled development that has taken place on so much of the coast. Furthermore, I would get to see my buddies again from Spain: Mody, Tom, Ian, Joe and Leo.

We agreed to meet at Lisbon Airport, and from there we traveled by van to Milfontes, a small village on the coast. This is where we met our hosts and owners of this operation, Robert and Sheila, who then drove us to their home and stables. We were served lunch there with a few more guests, including a couple from Germany. After lunch all the riders were taken down to the stables to examine our horses, which were pre-chosen for us. The horses were pure or cross-bred Lusitano.

The following morning for our get-to-know-our-horse ride we set off under cloudy skies. I was on a big tall gray Lusitano that gave me the toughest ride I'd ever been on. What happened was this: the horse hadn't been ridden for a few weeks and had an exceptionally strong mouth. I had very strong arms, but still could not control or stop this horse on a gallop. I call this type of horse a killer horse. And to top everything off, it started to pour rain, making my grip on the reins very slippery in my leather gloves. When we finally made it back to the stables, my arms and shoulders were sore. I told Sheila that I would require a stronger bit or a different horse. She chose a gallant-looking buckskin called Fashida for me that I enjoyed riding for the next ten days on our five hundred kilometer circle.

The following morning we were given a demonstration of what was required of all the riders. For example, after the day's ride was over, we were required to wash the bits, to cover each horse in the evening and to dismount and walk on foot for fifteen minutes before the lunch break and at the end of each ride. Furthermore, grooming was required twice daily. When we did finally start and came across a few short or long hills to climb, and even when going downhill, all riders were required to dismount and walk on foot, alongside their horse.

Nadine and Hy – Hotel Don Feiknandu, Portugal

After two days of this nonsense and exhaustion we North American riders decided to have a serious conversation with Sheila. She agreed to let us sit in the saddle on any hill we climbed provided we gave our word we would get our butts out of the saddle, and if not, the penalty was to dismount immediately. We agreed to her terms.

After riding through many small villages and towns, we came across oak and pine forests, across golden plains ablaze with wildflowers and then, finally, to the firm sandy beaches that gave us the widest variety of landscape and the most opportunities for trots and canters.

We then came to the thrill of a lifetime when we finally reached the "end of the world" at the Cape St. Vincent, and all the riders celebrated with champagne supplied by Robert and Sheila. From here we rode a short distance to Sagres, which is the furthest point west on the European continent. Up until the fifteenth century the people of Europe thought that this was the end of the world. When the New World was discovered, thousands of people would stand on the high cliffs and wave to the sailors passing by in their ships heading out to the Atlantic and eventually to the New World.

After taking this in, we moved on in an easterly direction to the city of Faro, and then northerly in a large circle heading back to Milfontes. Just before we reached our final destination, we were all offered a chance to compete in a jousting game. This was not against other riders, but a fun game where the riders were given long jousting poles and at a fairly good speed were required to pick off the rubber rings placed about twenty yards apart in a circular ring. The winner was determined by the clock and by how many hits he made going twice around the ring. I am pleased to report that my horse and I won the competition. No one was injured on this trip, and the young couple from Germany suggested that the next ride in Europe should be in Poland – that's right, Poland. She would make all the arrangements for traveling, and suggested we travel to Poland via Berlin by train, and that was, naturally, my next trip.

Shiela the owner with the writer – Portugal

Lunch time on the high cliffs

Jousting competition

137

# Chapter 28

For my trip to Poland, I was to meet my American friends at a hotel in downtown Berlin. Once reunited, we met up with some new riders: Mr. Steven Green, a rather wealthy businessman from Israel, his lovely girlfriend, Sonia, and Aurom from Zimbabwe, who was studying medicine in Great Britain.

We spent the evening in Berlin and, as we had prearranged train tickets in hand, we just had to eat breakfast and take two cabs to the train station. We were told that this was a ten-hour train ride with a stop at the Polish frontier for a customs check. I never thought that as a Canadian I would require a visa, nor did Mr. Green or his girlfriend Sonia.

At the customs checkpoint they took the three of us off the train in the pouring rain into what seemed to be a small jail. In Polish, they told us that we could purchase a visa right there provided we could pay in Polish zlotys, not U.S. or Canadian currency, or even German marks. The officers behind the desk told us not to worry, reassuring us that if the train left without us we could hail a taxi and catch the train at the next stop. How fortunate we were that Sonia understood and spoke Polish. We received our visas and the three of us set off in a taxi to chase down the train.

The next problem arose when we found that the auto didn't have working windshield wipers or a defroster. The driver could barely see, and at these high speeds we were reluctant to put our lives in danger. We asked the driver for a hotel, and to our surprise, he said that there was a Radisson Hotel not too far away in a city called Szczecin. Szczecin is one of Poland's oldest cities. Its origins date back to the ninth century when a heavily fortified castle was located on the site of what is now the palace of the Dukes of Pomerania. Szczecin, I learned, is a city of culture. In addition to its Philharmonic Orchestra, it has two theatres, a concert hall and art galleries.

That evening we went for dinner and Steve informed me that he could not continue on for the ride, as business in New York required him to leave immediately. Since I had no idea where I was heading, he checked the train schedule and found that I could leave at 9:00 A.M. Since he was holding the three tickets, he offered to see me off at the station. He told me not to worry as I was to get off at the last stop. Upon paying my bill, I changed my Canadian dollars to zlotys to meet any unexpected charges on the ten-hour ride.

Once on the train, I knew we were heading in a northerly direction, as one of the major stops was Gdansk, a shipbuilding city. The time seemed to go by quickly, and I found it interesting traveling on a Polish train. I noticed people drinking beer from large bottles and eating sandwiches, so I asked where I could buy drinks. I was told that there was a train car set up with tables, and a kitchen where food and drink could be purchased. After walking through a few cars I finally came to the "diner."

We finally got to the last stop and a young fellow came aboard looking for me. He helped me with my luggage, brought me to his vehicle, and off we went to the home base in a town called Dabrowa. I met up with our American group and the German couple who organized this trip at a local home. We all started to talk at the same time. First, they wanted to know, what happened to Steven Green and his girlfriend. I explained that he had to return because of business reasons. I wanted to know what I missed, and the group said that they were taken on a bus trip to the most western part of the U.S.S.R.

17 Hands & Spicy – Poland at Monastery

Our host

The most important part of that first evening together with my friends was meeting our host, a very gregarious large man with a full-grown beard, who spoke perfect English. Maerak was just a great guy, who constantly gave his best effort to please us. For example, he provided music each and every night at dinner. Vodka and beer were in ample supply at all times and wine was served at all our meals. There were a few evenings when he even arranged for a troupe of twelve musicians, folk dancers and singers to entertain us.

The following morning after breakfast, we all went to select the horses we intended to ride and arrived at an ancient barn that held about fifteen horses in very close quarters. In addition, there were five extra tall horses standing separately, all the same dark bay color. Maerak, in his deep voice, shouted, "Who wants to ride spicy horses?" Suddenly everyone stopped talking, and to break the silence I raised my hand and volunteered. Naturally, this gave me first choice of the tallest of the spicy five. Just because a horse is tall doesn't mean he is the best – it's just that I take a better picture on a taller horse.

I decided to call him Spicy and brought him out to a large courtyard. With all new or unknown horses, I have someone hold the horse's head while simultaneously pulling down hard on the outside stirrup as I get on, to avoid the saddle slipping under my two hundred pounds. As soon as I touched the saddle, I thought perhaps I made the wrong choice in taking on this spicy gelding. I immediately had trouble controlling him as he was trying to rear and was throwing a few bucks and tossing his head. I was just about to dismount when I noticed him fighting me and pulling hard on the bit to get me to his four other roommates. As I was approaching ever closer, he started to calm down, and I knew right then and there what his problem was. I asked Mody, Sean, Leo and his wife, Helga if we could ride together since my horse didn't appreciate riding without his buddies, and they naturally agreed.

Since we had a large group of riders, Maerak decided to split us up into two groups, which turned out to be a good idea. Our guide was a young woman who spoke very little English and understood even less. The horses were getting fidgety and anxious to move out when Maerak shouted that he wanted to give us some directions as soon as we all settled down. He explained that the route we were to take covered mainly agricultural ground, a few villages, and a monastery, where we were to spend the evening and sleep in the monks' quarters. He also mentioned that the area we were in was underpopulated with very little traffic on the roads, and a truck with horse supplies, as well as our luggage and drinks, would also be with us. Once everyone got organized, off we went, following our guide.

This Polish ride was very interesting for many reasons. Since we were riding through small villages and actually visiting the residents in their homes, we began to understand their frustrations with their lives. For example, first they had the Nazis to contend with for six years, then the Russians took over and stayed for another forty years. Poland was chosen by Adolph Hitler as the place to build his headquarters. *Wolfsschanze*, The Wolf's Lair, was built in the forest of Gierloz, eight kilometers from the town of Ketryzn, which I was able to visit. Not many tourists visit this site

Hitler's with staff

Göring's bunker

Bunker for main purposes

Hitler's bunker

Flak tower

since it is an area in far eastern Poland and quite difficult to find. Hitler's Wolf's Lair was built in an eight-square-kilometer forest and covered two and a half square kilometers.

The construction was entrusted to the Todt Organization and was built by two to three thousand workers. Altogether, some eighty buildings were constructed. The *Wolfschanze* was Hitler's largest headquarters and almost a complete town in itself. It boasted two airfields, power stations, a railway station, air purification plant, a water supply and drainage system, heating and an extensive communications center. In 1944, *Wolfschanze* housed over two thousand people, including three hundred army officers, over twelve hundred soldiers and drivers, mechanics, waiters, barbers, administration personnel, electricians, typists, etc. Construction started in 1940 and lasted until 1944.

Hitler himself spent a total of eight hundred days at the *Wolfschanze*. The first time he arrived there was on June 24, 1941, after his aggression had begun against the Soviet Union. The evacuation of *Wolfschanze* came violently. The Red Army took position less than one hundred fifty kilometers away in February, 1944, when they decided to blow up all the bunkers and totally destroy Hitler's headquarters in east Prussia, which he used to direct the Russian front. The destruction took place on the 24th of January, 1945, by German pioneers in order to deny its use to the Red Army who arrived three days later.

On the 20th of July, 1944, Colonel von Stauffenberg arrived, bringing with him a bomb in a suitcase to be activated by a chemical fuse in an attempt to assassinate Hitler. The bomb exploded as planned, but instead of killing Hitler, four other people were killed. For this act, Stauffenberg and almost five hundred Germans were sentenced to death. They were mostly hung or shot. Claus Schenk, Earl von Stauffenberg and his adjutant, von Haeften were executed by a firing squad led by Lieutenant Werner Schady. Many of those arrested were subjected to severe forms of torture. The Volksgerichtshof, whose chairman was the infamous Dr. Roland Freilsler, handled the prosecutions. Many of the arrestees died in concentration camps and many others took their own lives. Hitler himself expressed his wish for the conspirators to be executed by hanging and sentences of this type were carried out cruelly. The vengeance of the Nazis spread as far as the families of the accused; many wives and children were also incarcerated, including von Stauffenberg's children.

A commemorative monument was erected forty-eight years to the day after the attack. Three of von Stauffenberg's sons were present at the unveiling ceremony.

The Polish ride continued each day with new surprises and changing weather. Rainstorms would appear suddenly, and many times we had to do a fast gallop to get to cover and to avoid lightning strikes. One interesting afternoon, Maerak brought us to an enormous park that was home to thousands of deer and antelope – a sanctuary of sorts, as the park ranger's job was to catch and dehorn them. The ranger took us to the warehouse where all these horns were stored, and my guess is that I saw thousands piled up at least fifteen feet high.

All of our accommodations were comfortable and different each night as we slept in motels, fortresses, homes and, as I mentioned, in monks' quarters. The only problem I can remember was trying to use the telephone for long distance. My advice: forget it.

On the last evening, Maerak himself played the guitar and sang for us. Knowing that Joe Geller and I were Jewish, he gave us each two bottles of kosher vodka, which meant that we could drink it during Passover. He was certainly one of the better hosts that I've met during my horse travels.

The next morning we went to the train station for our trip back to Berlin. I stayed two nights in Berlin, which I found to be one of the largest cities in the world. Berlin is a great place for sightseeing, eating and entertainment. A flight back to Toronto ended this 1997 Polish Adventure.

# Chapter 29
## Returning to the Holy Land

There is a delightful town called Rishpon, just fifteen minutes north of Tel Aviv. In Rishpon, a young ambitious gentleman, Udi, owns and runs a prestigious riding academy called The Jockey Club. This club features excellent boarding facilities that are utilized by diplomats and Olympians. They board their horses there and their children take lessons on English saddles. The barns are enormous and airy, with each horse's stall equipped with large fans to keep the flies away and the horses comfortable. The outdoor ring is Olympic size, containing a variety of jumps, and has a covered seating area should visitors want to watch the horse shows. The horses are warm bloods and bred in Europe. I made the acquaintance of Udi back in 1997 when I took a six-month sabbatical to Israel and became a resident of that amazing country.

The first horse he chose for me was a large stallion called Zeppelin who would not let any mare pass him by without letting her know he was available. He was certainly a challenge for me to ride, especially when he decided he wanted to stop and not move any further. I learned that I required a riding crop whenever I took him out for rides among the orange, grapefruit and melon groves. I rode Zeppelin for two years until they shipped him out, as he was becoming a nuisance for the boarders who had mares.

The next horse I was given, in 1999 and 2000, was a Russian-bred thoroughbred named Mahogany, a bright chestnut with a flowing red mane. Mahogany was great to ride in the enclosed paddock, but once I took him out in the countryside, his personality quickly changed back into a racing horse, and since he had a strong mouth, he was tough to hold back. I needed to pull up with both arms. There are many horses who train on a regular basis in enclosed rings or corrals, and then when they are taken out into open fields, they can prove to be extremely dangerous, especially to youngsters who do not have the strength to stop a galloping horse. That's why it is of the utmost importance that children and adults wear approved safety helmets and breakaway stirrups that will allow the rider to fall free and not get dragged in the stirrups.

The only complaint I had riding in Israel during the summer months was the heat. The sun rises at 5:30 A.M. and stays up until 9:00 P.M. I must be saddled and on my way no later than 7:00 A.M., otherwise, between the flies and the scorching sun, it can become very uncomfortable.

Rishpon, Israel – 1999

# Chapter 30
# The Good Ol' U.S.A.

I was very fortunate when I met the group of American riders in Spain in 1988, as they were all members of the Mountain Patrol of San Mateo County. They invited me to join them on their fifty-first annual Fall ride, which took place in an area called Charity Valley. I understand that the Fall rides take place in a different area of California each year. Charity Valley is located just a few miles from the Nevada state line in central California.

The mounted patrol was formed in January 1942, immediately following the Pearl Harbor disaster of December 1941, and played an extremely vital role during the war years. San Mateo County has miles of rough, unprotected coastline and virgin country, accessible only on horseback. Vital war industries sprang up adjacent to the wooded areas, making constant patrolling a must. Thus, the Mounted Police of San Mateo County was born, having as its head the sheriff and the chief fire warden of the county.

Members of the Patrol are selected from residents of San Mateo, Santa Clara and San Francisco Counties who are interested in horsemanship to the extent that they are adequate horsemen themselves and are interested in furthering interest in

149

horsemanship in the area. These men must own their own horses and equipment and, before becoming members, must be invited on and attend at least six Mounted Patrol events, including one overnight ride. This experience better acquaints them with the Patrol and the Patrol with them.

It was not until 1947 that the tradition of the Fall ride began, when the yearly elections for captain where instituted. In June of 2002, I was invited on the California coast ride by members of the Mounted Patrol and was given a grand tour of their facilities. The Patrol owns twenty-two acres in the heart of Woodside, California. The location is in a spectacular area of mature trees, and their first-class clubhouse includes a large dining area, bar, offices and outdoor patios overlooking the professionally built horse show ring where the Patrol hosts the annual Nor-Cal Junior Rodeo every Fourth of July, along with many other horse shows and horsemanship clinics. The scenery is just spectacular and all riding trails have been prescouted to guarantee that the riding will be fantastic.

Woodside, which is a few miles south of San Francisco, is a horseman's paradise. Many people own horses here and stable them right behind their homes. I understand that to purchase a home in Woodside in 2002, one would have had to be prepared to pay at least one-and-a-half million dollars. The weather on the west coast is just ideal for all outdoor activities: riding, golfing, tennis, hiking and the ever-popular bicycle riding. This information may be interesting to any horseman contemplating moving to the San Francisco area in the near future.

The members of the Mounted Patrol are proud of the reputation that has been built up over the years as one of the finest organizations of its kind in the state. Each year finds them working to carry on and live up to this heritage. I understand that there are one hundred members who all take riding very seriously. The Mounted Patrol of San Mateo County are just a great bunch of guys, and even though they all knew that I was a guest from Canada, they gave me the royal treatment with a balance of humor, friendship, respect and comradery.

From left: Mody, (Harry), Tom, Joe
Members of Mounted Patrol of San Mateo County – 1999

151

## Chapter 31

# Returning to a Different Mexico

T om Smith, from the San Francisco area, received a call
from an old Mexican friend and fellow ardent horseman
to organize a small group to come to Mexico City and
go riding in their large national park. Tom told Joe Geller, and
Joe Geller told me. And, well, off we went. We met up with our
group at the Marriott Airport Hotel in Mexico City. The group
consisted of Joe, Tom and his second wife, my old friend, Dr. Jay
Smith, Leo and Helga, as well as some boys from the Mounted
Patrol. Our tour guide was Dr. Juan Agnasio Rodriguez, who
insisted we call him Nacho for short.

On the bus ride to San Miguel Regla, a magnificent resort
hotel just thirty kilometers from Pachuca, Nacho briefed us
about the trip over tequila, salt and lime. After dinner, where
we got acquainted with one another and listened to a terrific
Mexican professional orchestra, we went back to our villa-type
rooms and prepared for our first day out.

To some Americans this trip wasn't easy. Mexican saddles
have wooden seats, which are not entirely comfortable, and
when Nacho brought us back to the hotel in the dark, much
after 8:00 P.M., a few of the senior riders decided to return
immediately to Mexico City. I decided to stay on, and on the
second day, after being halted by heavy rain delays, I met the
owner of the Hacienda San Miguel Regla, Mr. Geramann, under
a plastic temporary shelter. I decided to ride back with him and
his girlfriend.

I noticed along the way that they were riding on what looked like quarter horses, both in fine condition. When I inquired where they came from, he secretly took me to his private stable where he introduced me to his wrangler for a better choice of horses. He explained that when a group of our size arrives, he prefers to supply horses from a rental stable and that explained their scrawny appearance.

I was delighted by the "upgrade," and later that evening, went to celebrate with Mr. Geramnn, his girlfriend and some more tequila. We drank and sang, accompanied by a trio of musicians at the hotel, and by ten o'clock he felt ill and had to retire for the evening. I didn't see him for days, until he called me to apologize for his behavior and to discuss business with me. He was an importer of air conditioning units from the United States and also owned a reputable restaurant in Mexico City, and was looking for an investor in a new project. He wanted to revitalize an old castle and turn it into an exquisite hotel/restaurant on approximately fifty acres near a very popular tourist site, the remarkable pyramids at Teotihuacan, just south of Pachuca. If I was interested, he would arrange for his son to pick me up on my day of departure from his hotel and drive me to the site. Since I was always open to a venture investment, I agreed to have a look for myself as to what he was talking about.

On the day of my departure from the Hacienda San Miguel Regla, his son pulled up in front of my suite driving a new Cadillac sedan and loaded up my luggage in the trunk. After saying good-bye to my friends, I was off with Michael. Michael was a well-educated young man who spoke English fluently. After a long drive over some rough Mexican roads, we finally arrived at the site. I wasn't overly impressed with what I saw, and even with cheap Mexican labor, the cost to renovate this project completely could run into the millions of dollars. I told Michael that there was a possibility that I might interest some investors in Canada to fly down and check out the site.

Since my flight back to Toronto wasn't until eleven that night, I accepted his invitation to lunch at his father's restaurant, located in a fashionable area and boasting some great dishes. After lunch, we drove to a combination art gallery and museum where he insisted I see a huge handmade wall decorated with inlaid precious stones. The wall rose up to twelve feet in height with a width of at least thirty feet. In the center was a most unusual fountain. I didn't realize why he wanted me to take such an interest in this wall until he drove me to his father's estate. The property was completely encircled with a fifteen-foot-high stone wall and the entrance was protected by two solid steel doors, with a private security force patrolling the perimeter of the entire property. After I entered this remarkable home, situated on ten acres, I was taken directly to the garden where Mr. Geramann was waiting for me and directed my attention to an exact replica of that same fountain wall. He was so proud of this wall and told me that it took the artisans over two years to duplicate.

After I had complimented him on the beauty of the wall, we went into his office to discuss any interest I might have had in investing in the renovation of the property that he had claimed he'd already purchased. I told him simply to fax me all his cost projections and what percentage of ownership he wanted me to have, and in turn, I would go to my business associates and if they liked the figures, we would be happy to fly into Mexico City and examine his site. As I expected, nothing came of this, and I never received a fax or a phone call.

He did furnish me with a limousine and driver for my return to the airport for my flight back to Toronto. Of course my American friends were anxious to learn about this great business deal and unfortunately I had to disappoint them in two words: no deal. A few weeks after returning home, I received a certificate from Dr. Rodriguez, stating that I had participated in the seven-day ride in Cabalgata Pachuquena de Mexico.

# Chapter 32
# The Hungarian General

I met my next group at the Marriott Hotel on the Danube in the great historical city of Budapest. In the evening I decided to take a stroll and was immediately targeted by the local prostitutes as a tourist. Perhaps it was the large belt buckle and western boots that I was sporting. I learned that the economy in 1994 was suffering and, as usual throughout the world, poverty breeds prostitution.

After an evening of Hungarian music and apple strudel in the lobby of the Marriott, I had no problem getting a good night's sleep, and in the morning I found a small restaurant that featured fresh bagels, New York-style. With an eye to the future ride, I went to the Marriott's outdoor bar and introduced myself to my fellow horse riders.

Again, I would be the only North American on the trip. The rest of the riders were from Germany, Belgium and Switzerland, a total of seven. Two autos came for our pick-up, and I was selected to ride with Marta, a very sweet and courteous young woman who spoke English very well. Most of the luggage was in our vehicle, and the other six passengers squeezed in with their driver, who was Marta's boyfriend. We drove in a northeasterly direction, and after approximately two hours arrived at our destination on the banks of the river Tisza. After dinner, there was an opportunity to dance to some wild Hungarian music from a six-piece orchestra.

At breakfast I met Janus, the owner and our guide, whom I nicknamed the General. Janus was thirty-five years of age and married. He owned his own riding academy where he specialized in dressage and jumping. Janus was short of horses, and at the horse selection he did not have a horse available for me and had to borrow one from a friend close to our hotel. The horse was a 16.2-hand-tall gray gelding called Lepke, who was to be my partner for the next two weeks. As Janus told me, his only fault was a fear of water and he did not enjoy crossing creeks and ditches. The first day out was quite nice as we had the opportunity to try our new steeds at walk, trot and canter. We were told that the following day we would be heading in the direction of the Czechoslovakian frontier.

The next day came quickly and it's one day I won't forget. Janus was in the lead. I was feeling good and the weather could not have been better – clear skies and just the right temperature for riding. I noticed a few of the women riders would ride up to Janus and have a conversation with him, however when I tried to ask him a few questions about the war years, he snapped at me to keep my distance as his horse might kick out. I fell back immediately, never to try that again. Later, we approached a wide ditch with running water that required the horses to jump over, and sure enough, Lepke was the only one to refuse. With Janus and the group staring and waiting for me to cross, I found it quite embarrassing trying to get my horse to cooperate and jump. It seemed like an hour, and Janus's screaming at me at the top of his lungs and barking orders for me to sit back in the saddle didn't help matters either. Finally, I leaned forward, talked gently and kicked as hard as I could. Sure enough, Lepke responded with a flying leap and landed on the opposite side. At that point I rode up to Janus and told him that in my country we lean forward to jump, and his reply was, "In your country and in America you are all cowboys on horses."

He was referring to the fact that the previous year he had my six friends from California, the ones from the thirty-day Spanish ride, who upset him because they were wearing western boots and not high English boots, and perhaps because they were also riding western style. In addition, one of the American riders received a strong kick that broke his leg bone when he couldn't stop his horse and had to be taken by ambulance to Budapest, at great expense to Janus. I believe that the incident cost his insurance company twenty-five thousand dollars, since the rider who was kicked was a lawyer.

After receiving that last insult, I didn't speak to Janus again until the last day of the ride. Again he barked and ordered me to put my boots back into the stirrups after I had removed them while waiting for a fellow rider to mount up. After a few more barked orders I finally told him that I was twice his age and he should show me some respect. I must admit, though, he was a talented rider and jumper and a knowledgeable man when it came to the management of his horses. However, when it came to his guests, he was a tyrant.

One morning at the outset of our ride, one of the women found her horse limping badly and immediately reported this to Janus. He lost his temper and blamed her for the horse's lameness and told her to dismount and walk the twenty-five miles at the side of her horse. This woman could not stop crying and pleaded that she was innocent and had done nothing wrong. After further examining the horse's leg, he decided to return to the stable where he found that the horse had been fed some very green alfalfa hay and that it was this that had caused the horse to become lame.

Another incident occurred during the second week when a new guest, Jacob from Switzerland, who was my roommate and a very genteel type of person, could not manage his horse on a very steep downhill grade and wanted to jump off and walk down. Janus screamed at him and ordered him to stay on, when suddenly Jacob lost his balance and fell hard to the ground. That's when I gave him the nickname "The Hungarian General."

The most memorable part of the ride was a visit we made to the area called Hortobagy, where I met some of the greatest horsemen in the world. These Hungarian cowboys gave us some demonstration of their skills. For example, they rode full gallop in the saddle without a girth holding the saddle in place. Try that sometime, and find out how difficult it is – but not at a gallop!

Last day in Gypsy Village

We also saw them round up a herd of approximately fifty horses at full gallop and steer them in different directions, then come to a quick halt without any fence to block them and hold their positions. We toured their stable and barn areas and then had dinner with these remarkable horsemen. Also, in the second week, I did some heavy trotting and galloping in the Puszta area, visited many vineyards and underground storage cellars with hundreds of large wooden barrels of wine and had the opportunity to taste many varieties of red and white Hungarian wines.

We dined in hunting lodges, private homes, outdoors and in a few castles. There were two other gentleman who participated in the two-week trip, both German chaps, Udo and Andre, who polished their boots daily. At the end of the trip, Marta offered to drive me to a town called Zeged, which I thought was where my father-in-law was from, provided that I take her mother to see Miss Saigon at the theater in Budapest. I had already seen it – but not in Hungarian. It was a deal.

The trip to Zeged was very interesting; every quarter of a mile we would see a dozen or so women on the side of the highway trying to get drivers to stop for afternoon pleasures. Zeged, in fact, was not the town my father-in-law was from. It turned out that his village was called Marmoresh Sïghet, in Transylvania. In any event, I was not disappointed as Zeged had many outdoor cafes. That evening I did take Marta's mother to the theater.

The following day, while walking about Budapest, I found by accident the Great Budapest Synagogue on Dohany Street, which is the largest in all of Europe. I understand that it can seat up to three thousand people. That same evening I said goodbye to Budapest.

I thought about this adventure with mixed feelings. I enjoyed my horse, the food and the famous gypsy music, however, I might have had a more pleasant horse trek if the Hungarian General had been more courteous to me and some of his guests.

The Dohany Utza Synagogue in Budapest

# Chapter 33

# The First Serious Accident

June 9th will always stand out in my mind, and ever since this accident happened in the year 2000, my mind always goes back to that date whenever I'm on a horse. It all started when my friend, Dan Capone, called me from New Jersey, looking for an overseas ride in early April of 2000. Since I knew that I was going to leave for Israel in May, I checked with Equitour and found a horse trek in Turkey that had an opening for a horse ride in early June. I checked with my son Mory and he said he could be available. His friend Jay also said he'd go and would ask the young lass from Belgium, Edith, whom he met at the Shively Ranch. We all agreed to meet at the Istanbul Airport on June 5th.

At that time I hadn't been to Turkey for at least five years, so I was pleasantly surprised upon landing in Istanbul from Tel Aviv to see a new, modern airport. I had only a short wait when the other riders arrived right on time. We were met by our Turkish guide and driven to our hotel in the old section of Istanbul, Sultanahmet, which was within walking distance of the Grand Bazaar. Ali, our guide, spoke perfect English and explained our itinerary to us. We would stay two nights in Istanbul with full sightseeing of this magic city of the Bosphorus, which is the strait between the Black Sea and the Sea of Marmara. Turkey is the only country in the world that is part of two continents, Europe and Asia. The ancient city of Istanbul was once the largest and mightiest in the world.

I will just mention a few of the sights we saw: the Grand Blue Mosque, Topkapi Palace and the Grand Bazaar, where we spent many hours and which has at least one thousand stores that sell everything from expensive jewelry, carpets, leather jackets, souvenirs, all types of clothing, hand bags, diamonds and gold. Tea is served to customers in small glasses with two or three sugar cubes on the side.

On both evenings we were taken to typical Turkish restaurants where we found the food and wine excellent – and the belly dancers weren't bad either. Ali told us that we were to fly to a city in central Turkey called Kayseri, named after the Roman Caesar, and from there we would take a three hour bus ride to Cappadocia, an area of the most unusual landscapes in the world. Cappadocia has been a meeting ground for European and Asian civilizations since long before the time of Alexander the Great. The ancient Greeks wrote of the fine horses raised there more than two thousand years ago, the ancestors of the animals we would ride through this fascinating region. Rich reminders of history were everywhere. The rock, which nature created in dramatic formations and in a variety of colors, can be easily worked and huge secret caves had been hallowed out where thousands of early Christians took refuge from Muslim invaders.

We finally came to our final destination, Avanos, a small town with one four-star hotel. We decided to make it our headquarters. The hotel was clean and had outdoor facilities for dining and we could eat our breakfast and dinner each day in the hotel. Also, we had the full-time services of a van and driver. We finally got to meet our host, Erican, who tried very hard to speak English and had a delightful location for his stables. He introduced us to two other adventurous souls who were to join us on a ride: a woman from America and a young, single European gentleman with long hair down to his shoulders who seemed to know Erican quite well. The first hour we spent sorting out which horses we were to ride, and the one picked for me seemed very thin and undernourished, and stood at 14.2 hands, which is short. Once we were saddled, we were told that there is no trotting; either we walk or fast gallop.

Cappadocia Ride – Turkey

This was to be a tryout run, but in the three hours we were out, I think we galloped more than two hours and my horse seemed to be tripping quite regularly. When we returned to the stables, I told Erican that I wasn't pleased with my horse, and he suggested that I switch horses with my son. Mory mentioned that he was pleased with his mount; he was taller and better built and gave him a decent ride – he could find no fault with him. Jay, Dan and Edith also said that their mounts were fine.

The following morning after breakfast, Erican said he would take us on a full-day ride into a mountain range behind Avanos where we would stop for lunch in a village called Ozkonak and visit the underground city hollowed out of rock. This was on June 9th. I was very pleased with my horse, who never stumbled once on the way to Ozkonak. We left our horses together in a small grassy area across from the small café where we had lunch. The sun was up and so was the temperature.

Suddenly we heard that Erican's horse broke away and took off. He managed to get a motorcycle rider to chase after his horse who, by the way, had no bridle or saddle. We had removed them from the horses during the lunch break, which is usually a good idea. After fifteen minutes, the seven of us stood watching as we saw a white horse galloping toward us at full speed, with Erican on his back holding on to the horse's mane, with no control to stop or slow the horse. What happened next was that Erican went flying off the horse when the animal plowed into a mound of rocks just above where the other horses were grazing. Erican landed on his wrist and you could see that he was in great pain, although he insisted that he was all right.

We saddled our horses quickly for the return ride to Avanos, which was downhill through a rocky canyon. We had a choice to stay in the saddle or walk alongside our horses down the rocky trail. No one seemed to want to dismount. When we were only about four kilometers from the stables, suddenly without notice of any kind, my horse went down on both front legs at the same time, followed by his hind legs, which thrust me to the left side of the horse and onto a hard rock surface. I hit the ground quick and hard, breaking my collarbone, which was sticking out through my shirt. Had this been my forehead hitting the ground, I probably would have been brain damaged or in a coma. This all happened in seconds and since Jay was directly behind me he witnessed the horse collapse on his four legs at virtually the same time. I must have had hundreds of horses trip, stumble and slip under me but never, ever had a horse gone down on all four legs at once. I decided to walk back to the stable, but after fifteen minutes in the heat and in pain I gave up. Erican then galloped ahead to get a vehicle to fetch me.

I could have sworn that the first hospital they brought me to was an abattoir, with two heavy-weight nurses coming at me wearing aprons completely covered in blood. I could also see that the walls and floor hadn't been washed in months. Ali translated and advised me that this hospital had no x-ray equipment and the best they could do for me was give me some pills to lessen the shock.

Ali suggested that we go to a private doctor's hospital in a city called Nevschir, twenty miles from Avanos. There I was given quick attention and the head surgeon ordered x-rays immediately. After viewing them and speaking to Ali and my son, I heard the

Cappadocia Injury – Turkey

news: I required immediate surgery. That evening I was told to remove my boots and riding clothes so that certain tests could be taken before surgery. Erican was also there and requested that they check his wrist. It was found to be broken and required a cast. At least this hospital seemed civilized, very clean and the nursing staff's uniforms were immaculate.

That evening I went under the knife for the first time in my life. It was explained to me that the surgeon would insert two large pins to hold the bone in place and that I must wear a sling for the next six months, not moving my arm in any way. Being right-handed, I was at least fortunate to break my left shoulder, and also to have my son there to help me get dressed and undressed, tie my laces and do up my belt and many other favors that a one-handed man requires. After two nights in the hospital, I went to the office to pay the hospital bill by Visa.

When my son and I were about to leave, we saw Edith being carried in on a stretcher with Jay by her side. We were told that the horse she had been on that morning slipped on a cement slab somewhere near the stable and fell over on his side, trapping Edith under him. Evidently, her ankle took the full brunt of the accident and she required x-rays to determine the extent of the damage. What a shock that was, to see her carried in on a stretcher, and even more of a shock to learn later that she had had a serious break and her ankle required a cast up to her knee for at least three months.

We still had four days of our horse vacation left, and with two down, there were still three riders out of the group left to enjoy themselves. I depended heavily on Ali to keep me busy. To my surprise, he told me that he was the proud owner of Ali Safran hand-crafted rugs and that his factory and store were just a few miles from Avanos, in a village called Goreme. So that is where I spent some time, sipping tea and checking out the rugs. I actually purchased a fifteen-foot runner that took six months to arrive in Canada. I also managed to ride with the van's driver, who didn't speak a word of English, to meet up with the riders for lunch. And, finally, our group, without Edith, was taken to a typical Turkish bathhouse for a hot steam and massage. Edith was having problems walking on crutches and not being able to put any weight whatsoever on her broken ankle.

The ride finally came to an end, and we departed Avanos for the van ride back to Kayseri and the flight to Istanbul. Jay and Edith decided to stay near the airport at the five-star Marriott as she could not walk or move about very well. Dan, my son and I stayed at the same hotel as before, close to the Bazaar, so we could do some last minute shopping. At the Istanbul Airport we said our good-byes, with Dan flying off to the U.S.A., Mory, Jay and Edith flying off to Belgium and I to Tel Aviv, where I got an earful from my wife about my accident.

Eventually, I went to an orthopedic surgeon for further x-rays and was told that the surgery I had in Turkey was outdated by about twenty years. That was confirmed six months later by my surgeon in Toronto who operated on my shoulder to remove those long, ugly pins they had inserted. After many months of therapy and exercise, all my arm movements are back to normal. I must stress the fact that anyone riding a horse, whether child or adult, should wear a certified helmet for protection.

The worst part about the accident was that I had to give up riding for almost an entire year. To regain my confidence, I made two separate trips to the TX Ranch. The last trip, in late April of 2002, was with my daughter, who was the last of my children to visit the TX. The TX horses have such superb strength and never let you down, and I was able to ride at my own speed whenever and wherever I pleased.

I have to give my daughter Nadine, who is thirty-nine and has three children, and my daughter-in-law Debra credit for putting up with the hardships at the TX. First of all, the weather was not cooperative; it snowed for two days and the temperature went below freezing. Nadine and Debra never complained and I am proud of them. The Tillets finally got to meet all of my children, my five sons and my daughter. I am now hearing rumors that my grandchildren are going to ask me to take them on the next cattle drive in Montana.

My first serious accident – Turkey

# Chapter 34
# A Few Potentially Dangerous Riding Experiences

Horseback riding is not only a physical sport, but can also be dangerous at times, since the experience is shared with an animal. For example, riding with a small group at the TX ranch in Montana, with Hip's sister Latana as our guide, we lost our way up a mountainside. She was doing her best to find our way back when we got into a heavy forest on the side of an extremely steep hill. The going was tough on the horses and I was leaning forward as far as I could in the western saddle. At the same time, I could feel my horse straining to climb the higher we got. The hill seemed to go straight up. Then it happened; my horse started to fall backward, and fearing a serious accident, I quickly jumped down just as he started to fall down the slope. He was stopped by a couple of trees standing close together and not injured, but to get to the top, another fifty yards, I decided to walk on my own two feet with the horse directly behind me. That was really a close call.

Another close call occurred one winter on my farm when the children weremuch younger and I had all of them on a toboggan. They wanted me to pull them while sitting on my favorite horse, Joe. I made a terrible error by tying the toboggan's rope to my right wrist. Everything was fine and I was pulling the children through the snow, when suddenly the toboggan hit a gatepost, spooking Joe. He wanted to take off with the post holding the toboggan, and my right arm – with the rope tied to my wrist – being pulled from its socket. He thought he was in danger! There was no way I could hold him back and my only chance of avoiding serious injury was to get out of the saddle – and quick. This taught me a good lesson: don't ever tie a rope to any part of your body while working with horses. If you tie, you could die. Instead, just hold on to the rope with your hand and if anything startles the horse, just let go.

Anyone familiar with the Woodbine Race Track at the northwest area of Toronto knows how large the grounds are, with enough empty space to fill ten empty football fields. It was here that I managed to ride my horse, during an off-season period, keeping away from the barn and track areas. It was a pleasant day until a gang of loose dogs decided to attack my horse while I was in the saddle. I will never forget the look in the eyes of some of those German shepherds, dobermans and rotweilers. They had the look of demons ready to devour the horse and me. They all immediately attacked the horse's heels, and then a few jumped up to grab at my boots. A rotweiler got a grip with his teeth on my horse's rump, making him kick, buck and even rear slightly. A horse's natural instinct is to run when he feels threatened and after what seemed like ten minutes he did just that, leaving the pack of dogs far behind, running after us. My greatest fear was that if the horse had bucked me off I would definitely have been viciously attacked and perhaps unable to defend myself. My horse did have a bite on his right hind leg that required the attention of a veterinarian, including rabies and tetanus shots. I still can't figure out where that pack of dogs came from.

# Chapter 35

## *Conclusion*

**B**eing involved with horses over the past fifty years has brought me the opportunity to travel throughout the world as well as to meet other riding enthusiasts. Most significant to me is the enjoyment I get from this great sport of riding – the horse has brought both excitement and adventure into my life. It is difficult to explain the pleasure I've had, for most of my adult life, in riding and caring for these wonderful animals. I am now looking forward to training a three-year-old gelding registered quarter horse that my six children surprised me with on my seventy-fifth birthday in 2003.

# 𝕿𝖍𝖊 𝕭𝖆𝖎𝖑𝖞 𝕿𝖊𝖑𝖊𝖌𝖗𝖆𝖕𝖍

| 10 cents | Saturday, June 21 2003 | R.S.V.P. by JUNE 6/03 |
| --- | --- | --- |
| | | Nicki @ (905) 792-9898 |

## *Wanted: Dead or Alive*

Festivities begin at 3 pm !

**Harry's 75th Birthday Bash !!**

Please join us in celebrating Harry's

*75th Birthday Bash*

Saturday June 21, 2003

*at the BURSTEIN RANCH*

Caledon, Ontario

*Sheriffs & Deputies*
*Sonny & Galia*
*Mory & Debra*
*Dean & Rona*

*Dinner & Dancing*

*Dress: Western/Casual*
*Cowboy Hats: optional*

*take a hay ride...*
*play tennis...*
*ride a horse...*
*cool off in our pool...*

75th Birthday Bash at the Burstein Ranch – June 21st, 2003

I feel so fortunate that I have been blessed with six wonderful children, all accomplished riders. We all ride together on our farm just outside of Toronto, appropriately named Gan Eden Farms, which in English means the Garden of Eden. It has a landscape of high hills, forests and dense bush and a winding river, with our home sitting back six hundred feet from a private entrance off the main road. The stone driveway cuts through a dense forest, slowly exposing the beautiful expanse. The house was built in 1961, and has recently been restored to its former glory, with huge windows framing the magnificent view. The tennis court and swimming pool add flavour to the attractive property. My enjoyment, of course, is in the cozy barn, reached only by crossing a wooden bridge over the fast flowing river. Our barn is aesthetically completed by a large corral and riding ring, and our six horses enjoy a wonderful lifestyle by having complete freedom to roam our fully-fenced farm.

Throughout the years, my wife, Zuzik, a former Miss Israel and a finalist in the Miss World contest, has stayed as beautiful as the day I married her in Israel in 1959. Thanks to her encouragement, I started writing this book on the subject I love most – horses. It was also my wife who supported my need to travel to the far-off countries mentioned in the book, while looking after and caring for our six children. To you, Zuzik, I dedicate this book.

Burstein farm

171

# Afterword

I have just received a page from the U.S. magazine Trail Blazer, from my good friend from New Jersey, Mr. Dan Capone, describing the marriage of Lari Shea of the Richochet Ranch to Harvey, one of her guests on her Kenya ride, back in 1990. I knew at the time that there might be a romance shaping up, and even though it took eleven years to end in marriage, I am very happy for the both of them. Even though I never did receive an invitation to their wedding ceremony, I wish them both a happy mazel tov! I rode with Harvey and Lari again in Australia in 1991 and in the photo entitled "Four Veterans from Kenya," you will note Lari hanging onto Harvey's shoulder.

Four Veternas from Kenya (Ruth, Hy, Lari & Harvey)

The following poem was written by Diana Hunt Westa, and the title "The Aging Rider" describes who this poem was written for

# The Aging Rider

*When nerve and muscle no longer obey*
*The eager spirit - there comes a day;*
*When courage gives way to caution, and you*
*Begin to find reasons not to do;*
*When high adventure has lost its zest*
*Then its time for a reckoning - what is best?*
*So hark, young friends, as I tell it to you,*

*For surely at last you will be here too.*
*We flew that wall, the mare and I,*
*Now suddenly we pass it by:*
*Was it not just the other day?*

*She pricks her ears - I turn away.*
*Must all that joy belong to the past?*
*Is there nothing left to make it last?*
*Perhaps a way can yet be found -*

*Yes, there must be a lesser middle ground.*
*The call of the woods, the glow of the ride -*
*Slower, of course, and with shortened stride.*
*But the sun still warm and the water gleams*
*As ripples flow down the tumbling streams;*
*The wind blows fresh and spirits mend,*
*With your horse for companion - that*
*Comforting friend.*

# *Prayers from a Horse*

### *1.*

*Give me the time to know what you want of me.*
*I don't understand your words.*

### *2.*

*Don't be angry with me when I do not understand.*
*I have only you to explain things to me.*

### *3.*

*Talk to me.*
*Even if I don't understand your words,*
*I understand your voice.*

### *4.*

*be aware that however you treat me,*
*I will not forget.*

### *5.*

*Keep me safe from harm,*
*because I am no longer wild and able to know my enemies.*

### *6.*

*Before you hit me, remember that I have teeth*
*that crush the bones in your hand*
*and hooves that could kill you.*
*But I choose not to use them.*

### *7.*

*Before you scold me for being lazy or uncooperative,*
*ask yourself if I am ill or if something may be bothering me.*

## 8.

*My life is likely to last 20 to 30 years.*
*Please make sure that I am taken care of because*
*I cannot care for myself.*

## 9.

*Go with me on difficult journeys.*
*Don't say " I can't stand to watch it,"*
*or "let it happen in my absence."*
*Everything is easier for me if you are there.*

## 10.

*Place your trust in me and I trust you.*


*-Anonymous*